RED EAGLE
THE RED STICK WAR IN ALABAMA

Also by Peachill:

Barka: Lion of Carthage
Inca: The Golden Sun
1453: The Last Days of Constantinople
Empress Wu: Rise

RED EAGLE
THE RED STICK WAR IN ALABAMA

peachill

Peachill Publishing
Chapel Hill | New York | Santa Monica
www.peachill.com

Copyright © 2017 Peachill Publishing LLC

Peachill Publishing asserts the moral right to be identified as the author of this work

A catalogue record for this book is available from the US Library of Congress

All rights reserved. No part of this publication may be reproduced, stored in a retrieval system, or transmitted, in any form or by any means, electronic, mechanical, photocopying, recording, or otherwise, without prior permission of the publisher.

PROLOGUE

The Holy Ground

A scream shocked the grassland. Then another, and another, until the wind fell silent in fear. Eyes split wide open with panic until they were frozen by the specter of horrible death. All around, men screamed in agony as they watched life rush from them in red. The lucky ones—the ones whose bones were shattered by blunt weapons—didn't know how lucky they were. It's hard to count your blessings over the sound of your own deafening scream. A chorus of anger charged the field toward the enemy barricades. This was the Holy Ground no more.

Andrew Jackson, the angriest of them all, sat tall in the saddle, watching for any sign that his men were wavering, any sign that he should hate them, too. He itched to step in and lead the attack. He wanted blood. Whenever the smell of gun smoke filled the air, roused by the bark of rifles all around him, he always wanted blood.

A cannon roared to his left. Then, another. Logs splintered, sending fragments of native charms flying everywhere. The artillery thundered into the Indian camp on the plateau above, but there weren't nearly enough screams from the damn savages.

"General, sir," Captain Harding tugged at the reins of Jackson's horse. "If you could dismount, please. Red Eagle's the best shot on the battlefield."

"Is that the son of a bitch?" Jackson pointed at a tall, leanly muscular man crouched in the gateway at the top of the rise. As Jackson watched, smoke burst from the man's rifle and one of his soldiers fell a hundred yards away.

"No, sir," Harding said. "That's him." He pointed at a grey horse galloping down the hill toward them. The man on its back was paler than Jackson expected, but his dark hair and piercing eyes felt every bit as vicious the rest of the Creek braves.

The battle was pure chaos, just as Jackson had planned. Their sudden appearance had sent the Red Stick Creek rebels down the slope in reckless abandon, straight into the volley of American gunfire. Now they were fighting in broken groups, their frenzied brutality scattered across the edge of the woods. They fought with wild abandon, hacking frantically with axes and clubs, even when they were surrounded by certain death. There was a wildness in their eyes, but Jackson did not see it on the face of Red Eagle. He plowed straight through the line, hacking left and right, trailed by a red shadow of his destruction. All the while, his face had a patient ferocity that Jackson could not help but admire. It also frightened him to the core.

"If any man can beat us, it's that one," Jackson said.

"I agree, sir. He's lost too much to give up. Beware the caged animal."

"Beware me," Jackson drew his sword. "Come, Captain

Harding. I don't care if you burn down every Creek village in Alabama, but you'll have to cut the head off that Indian to win this war."

CHAPTER 1

Name Your Price

Several Years Earlier

Red Eagle paused for a moment, one hand holding a brush, the other resting on the shoulder of his horse. The forest had fallen silent for the briefest moment as the sun emerged from behind the clouds, its warm light gleaming like silver ribbons on the surface of the Coosa River. Above, the canopy glowed emerald as the light danced through the leaves. He closed his eyes and inhaled deeply. When the winter storms punished the homestead, he would remember this scent. Alabama in sunshine. That was all the hope he needed.

Turning his head, he looked toward the other light in his life, the brightest one. His wife sat in a chair outside the door of the timber-framed trading post, a shawl wrapped around her shoulders, one breast bared to feed their newborn baby. Sapoth looked as beautiful as the day they met. Her face was soft, and her figure still stirred a fire within him. Her hair, long and dark, draped down the sides of her face. Sensing his eyes on her, she looked up from the infant and smiled. Eagle's heart soared. All was right in the world.

A whistle whipped Red Eagle's attention back to the river. A canoe raced downstream toward him, a small pilot's paddle thundering a quiet storm. As the boat neared the bank, the paddler leaped onto land and plucked the canoe onto the shore. His clothing, weathered through repeated use, moved rigidly. It was an excessive amount of clothing for this weather, and Red Eagle recognized him because of it. Hide trousers, a sleeveless tunic of thin leather, feathers in his hair, and three sacred charms of cloth and bone dangling from a cord around his neck. Wearing light cotton pants and a shirt with buttons, Red Eagle stood in stark contrast. Who else would dress in such opposition but his brother?

"Red Eagle!" The man tossed his oar into the canoe with a clatter, sweeping his long hair to the side.

"Josiah," Red Eagle smiled, embracing his half-brother, resting his chin for a moment on top of the other man's head. Josiah reeked of herbs. A medicine man, the thick bouquet of his many healing plants always followed, but the leaves for smoking stood above. "You come to trade?"

Josiah let go and walked past Red Eagle, leaving wet footprints on the red clay track that ran beside the river. Red Eagle followed him with long, slow strides.

"In part," Josiah's charms rattling as he walked. "But other matters first."

Sapoth stood as Josiah approached and the two of them hugged, the baby clasped between them. Stepping back, Josiah looked down with a smile at the infant.

"At last you have made me an uncle!" he exclaimed. "My heart beats like a drum."

"Some little friends back at the Square Ground," Sapoth said, "would not be pleased you forgot about them so soon."

"Ah, but they are not Red Eagle's children. What is the special one's name?"

"We haven't decided. But it's all we talk about."

"This is your fault, isn't it?" Josiah turned to Red Eagle, his tone a mocking imitation of anger. "You have left my poor nephew without a name!"

"We want to give him two names to honor both his bloodlines," Red Eagle said, "but I didn't think it would be this hard."

Extending one finger toward the baby, Red Eagle watched in wonder as tiny pink fingers closed around his sun-browned skin. The soft warmth of that touch made him smile anew, as did the gurgle that followed.

"He doesn't look like your father," Josiah said. "Why inflict a European name upon him? We will gladly give him one of our own."

"He will have names from both his people," Red Eagle suppressed his annoyance. Just once, he wanted a visit from his brother without the deafening push of politics. Red Eagle, himself, was half white. Josiah, and anyone else for that matter, could plainly see it, and even though Red Eagle had chosen a wife from his mother's people, and lived by many of their ways, Josiah behaved as if their entire way of life was Scottish. Red Eagle's life was Muscogee, the same as Sapoth and Josiah. But his life was also European, like the Americans. He wanted this to be true for his son as well. Balance is the key to a full life.

Balance wasn't so simple, however. Not when local tribes,

the natives to these sacred lands, were increasingly affected by their European neighbors. Their clothes, their homes, and their beliefs were all mixing with foreign influences. That was no bad thing. Even a bull could see that hide trousers went better with a cotton shirt than with more leather. Red Eagle's house, the one his father built, was the sturdiest he had ever seen, the marriage between Alabama trees and Scottish technique.

Nevertheless, there was a growing divide, and not just between European and Muscogee. The Muscogee themselves had split between the Upper and Lower Creeks. The Lower assimilated progressively with their European trading partners. The Upper Creeks, to which Josiah held, made a point of upholding traditional Muscogee life and shunning everything else.

Red Eagle lived between the two for a reason. For one, he had no desire to play the game of marking territories. He was no dog. For another, the success of his trading post depended on it. He was independent, a friend to all, an enemy to no man, and he intended to keep it that way.

Breaking his gaze from the babe, Josiah looked to his brother in dramatic silence.

"You come from the blood of chieftains," Josiah said. "Your father may have watered down that legacy, but you are still respected among the tribes."

He spoke softly, but there was animosity in that tenderness, and it screamed across his stiff body. Choosing a white man meant their mother had left the tribe behind, and with it, her firstborn son. Josiah never forgot. No one would ever let him, for Muskogee tradition forever linked a child to their mother, so when she left him with his uncle, it was a moment burned in his memory. It was a truth Red Eagle knew all too well.

"It's good to hear our people respect me," Red Eagle said. "So do the Europeans, and the same will be for my son."

"I'm afraid that won't happen," Josiah looked out across the horizon above the river. "War is coming, as the Wind has long said it must. There is no peace for our people while—"

"Did you come here to lecture me on politics?" Red Eagle asked. "Let us go inside and discuss other matters—unless you hate to ruin your Muscogee body with the white man's coffee?"

"The rain may soak us, but it also helps the corn to grow." Josiah grinned, the hint of anger flickering out of his eyes. "Lead the way to the coffee."

Inside his trading post, Red Eagle used a hand mill to grind the coffee beans to a coarse powder. He put a kettle on the stove, while Josiah looked through the room for supplies. In exchange for the elk skins he brought, he sought beans, knives, and gunpowder. Normally, Josiah wasn't one for coffee, and partook only to humor his younger brother. The acidic drink was too bitter for his taste. But as Red Eagle ground it, the smell filled the room. Josiah grabbed a small sack from the shelf.

They sat for a while, trading sips for stories. The events in Josiah's world—who had married, whose children were born, which tribes were arguing over hunting grounds—had a curious habit of always changing, but never being different. Red Eagle's gossip came from further afield—business deals in Huntsville, politics in Washington, states forming and joining the Union. Again, Red Eagle tried to engage his brother in talk of philosophy and history—concepts he read in Caesar's *Gallic Wars* or other philosophical pamphlets brought by a French merchant. Each time, Josiah refused it as "foreign talk."

"Do not become too attached to such things," Josiah said. "Changes are coming, brother. The more you love, the more you will have to lose."

"I cannot choose what to love any more than I can choose what should not break."

"Bad blood is growing between our people, Red Eagle. The Spanish have agreed to provide guns for us. We seek a safe place to store them on their way up from Pensacola. This trading post is a good location for-"

"No," Red Eagle's brow stiffened to settle the topic out of the gate. "I am an open merchant. Goods for sale, not for smuggling."

Outside, the horses whinnied and ran across their paddock as the clopping of hooves and creaking of wheels announced another arrival.

"I should go," Josiah gathered his goods and headed for the door.

"There is no hurry." Red Eagle followed him.

Outside, a grizzled white man in his forties descended from the seat of a wagon. He and Josiah watched each other tensely for a long moment, and then the new arrival turned his attention to Red Eagle.

"Afternoon, Mister Weatherford," he said.

"Hello, Jim," Red Eagle replied, shifting from the Muscogee language to English. "And, please: call me William."

Josiah scowled but said nothing as he headed for his canoe.

"Right you are, William." Jim McKee walked around to the back of his wagon. "I've brought more corn and beans, like you asked. Tools too. And some new cloth dyes. Figured the folks out in the woods might like to make life a little more colorful."

The White Man knew not of his mistake. The forests were a patchwork of reds and greens, dotted with flowers in blue and yellow. The Breathmaker gifted a thousand silvers and blues in a single river. Some men were blind to color unless it was on their clothes, but the tribes knew full well that nature held the best palette.

"I don't have enough to trade for all of this," Red Eagle assessed the contents. "I have not seen as many furs as I hoped."

"Don't you worry about it," McKee said. "We'll work out what you can and can't cover. You'll make it up to me, I'm sure."

The thought made Red Eagle uncomfortable. He disliked being indebted. But he was right, these goods would make him a profit when the Creek came to trade. He glanced over to Sapoth, sitting on the porch with their beloved future in her arms. The baby started to cry and Sapoth stood up, whispering in his tiny ears to soothe him to sleep. Red Eagle looked back at McKee, who shrugged his shoulders.

"You would trust me like that?" he asked.

"Put 'er this way," McKee slapped him on the shoulder and gave a gap-toothed grin. "Everyone knows they can trust William Weatherford."

Together, they unloaded the wagon, and, as Red Eagle

tried to hide his concern about his wailing future, a hideous opossum scurried into the woods.

CHAPTER 2

The Old Man's Song

As Red Eagle clasped the last pannier beneath his horse, the door swung open with a squeak. Sapoth stood outside, their infant son wrapped to her breast. It was noon on a beautiful day that just got brighter. She wore a traditional Creek dress, which made him suddenly aware of his clothing, his saddle, his fair skin. She was beautiful any time of day, but now, when the light caught her hair dancing in the sunshine, everything seemed to slow as if time itself was pausing to admire her beauty.

Floating down the stairs, she embraced Red Eagle before he helped her onto the horse. Having his family with him would make this a slow ride. Looking at Sapoth's face, all his worries were put to rest. One look at that smile told him everything he needed to know. They were going, no matter how long it took to get there, and they were excited about it.

Red Eagle led his horse, and his family, away from their homestead toward the *Puskita*.

∼

The murmur of human voices echoed down from the tree

canopy above. They were finally getting close. Excited cries, raucous laughter, the beat of a drum. Jubilation on the horizon.

Emerging in the openings between the trees, the grand Muscogee Township spread out before them. Rings of outer clan houses led all the way to the opposite side of the Square Ground. They were barely past the first house on the edge when Onawa spotted Sapoth and rushed to pull her off the horse.

"Sapoth, where have you been?" Onawa asked. "Where are your ribbons? Broken Tree has twice called for the dance!"

With a smile, Sapoth handed Red Eagle their child with a kiss on the cheek. Hopping from the back of the horse, she ran off at Onawa's heels. Before disappearing around the corner, she froze, looked back, and smiled. Red Eagle did not mind.

His mother taught him the importance of tradition to the Creek people, but he was the living embodiment of change. He was part of this family, but whenever he was around them, he felt separate. It didn't help that children would point and stare. He didn't regret the life he chose to live with Sapoth. He took pride knowing theirs was a love uniquely their own. But the specter of tension between the two sides within him felt particularly vulnerable in this climate. It wasn't as if Josiah would give him the benefit of the doubt.

An offering was the only option to announce his arrival. He was not fasting, but he would show his respect. He stopped to dismount the horse near the Square Ground. Reaching into his saddle pack, he took the offering and laid it behind the eastern arbor. Nearby, the feast was being prepared. The old fire, the dwindling flame of the last harvest, still burned in the center of the Square. He looked around and, to his surprise, no one was staring at him. Then again, they had been fasting for several days and only had eyes for food. He'd have to fake his own suffering to blend in.

Red Eagle returned to his horse and scooped up his son. He wondered how curious it all must look to him. It was his first trip to the Muscogee Township, and he was the blood of a Wind clan chief. One day, he would understand all that it meant. For now, a tour from his father would have to do. Circling the elevated Square, Red Eagle patted his hand on the dirt walls.

"We lift our Square Ground toward the sky to show respect to the Breathmaker, who gives us life," Red Eagle whispered to his son. "And each side points in a different direction to honor all to whom we owe thanks."

A firm but shallow voice called out from within the Square.

"I call again, a third time, for the Dance of Ribbons."

Red Eagle would recognize that voice anywhere. He turned to see Broken Tree, his great uncle, standing across the way. Once a force of pure intimidation, the large man stood smaller than Red Eagle remembered. The plume of feathers in the bonnet extended above his long gray hair. When age takes its toll, it is possible to accept it gracefully. Red Eagle was thankful to make it in time for the last night of the celebrations, and joined the tired and hungry moving toward the fire. He lifted his son high into the air to survey the scene.

"This is called '*Puskita*.' This time every year, we celebrate renewal for man and woman, and give forgiveness to everyone and everything. This enables new growth."

Red Eagle turned away from the Square and walked along a row of clan houses to the East.

Rounding a corner, Red Eagle caught a surprised Josiah, sitting cross-legged on the grass between two houses. A black pot of ash sat in front of him.

"My eyes deceive me," Josiah said evenly. "My brother Red Eagle could not possibly stop his work to celebrate."

Josiah drew a knife against the skin of his arm. The feathering barely makes a scratch, calling the slimmest film of blood to the surface.

"You remember your uncle Josiah," Red Eagle looked to his son. "He is a man of the old ways."

"And that makes you a man of the new ways, brother?"

Red Eagle smiled. This was his brother, alright.

A flap opened on the clan house beside them, and out streamed six women, laughing in the dusk air. Bright and clean, they wore cotton skirts with patterned tunics, and ribbons in their hair.

"Come, brother," Red Eagle gestured toward the Square. "Time to clean ourselves of last year's fire."

"You have your path, Red Eagle. And I mine."

Josiah reached into the black pot and removed a handful of white ash from last harvest's fire, smearing the ash all over his face, down his neck, then all over his body.

Red Eagle followed the women toward the Square.

∽

Red Eagle propped his son up on his lap, facing the Square.

Sapoth carved a graceful path through the crowd of women, moving her feet to the beat of her shaker. It was light, but steady, and sure of itself. Ribbons danced behind her the entire way.

"This is how I fell in love with your mom," he whispered to his son.

Sapoth closed her eyes, but kept her dance open. Twirling the ribbons in her fingers, she swung her arms upward, before plunging them down her sides, spinning to the music. Red Eagle couldn't look away.

The beat rolled on, each dancer moving to her own rhythm. Some fast, some slow. Some with vigor, Sapoth with grace. The dancers curled near the old fire, and the first dancer ripped a ribbon from her vest and cast it into the flames.

"Every ribbon is a prayer," Red Eagle told his son.

Unlike other women, Sapoth did not rip any ribbons from her clothes to cast them into the fire. She kept them all. What was she waiting for?

With one sudden call, Broken Tree's voice broke his trance.

"It is time for the Stomp Dance."

The exodus of ribbon dancers left a lone figure in the center of the Square. Broken Tree pulled a tobacco pipe from his belt, packing it before lighting it with the final flames of the old fire. Slow and steady, he took a large, deliberate pull before the smoke escaped his lips, floating upward into the Great Mystery. All around, eyes waited until it was time. After the seventh pull, Broken Tree turned and walked north for the river. Red Eagle followed along with the rest of the men.

Settling on the river bank, Broken Tree passed the pipe to

his second chief, Menawa, a mountain whose pulls sounded like roars. After his seven, he passed it down the line to the heads of each Clan before it landed again in Broken Tree's hand.

"Wind clan," he announced, staring at Red Eagle.

Unsure if that was an invitation or a reprimand, Red Eagle stepped forward. When the pipe found his hand, it seemed to have a power all its own, finding his gaze and trapping it within. He exhaled and pressed his lips to the pipe, puffing the sacred herb in round pulls. He then passed it to his medicine man brother to close the circle.

As Josiah smoked his seven circles, Broken Tree looked to the sky, and held up his arms toward the Breathmaker.

"Who will lead our Dance of Spirits?" he asked.

Dusk had swallowed the sun. Only the moon was left in its wake, kissing the outlines of the clouds in indigo. Silence. Broken Tree again raised his hands to the sky.

"Must the Dance have a leader as in years' past?"

The wind rustled across the leaves beyond the river as Josiah continued huffing on the pipe. A "Yes" from the Breathmaker.

"Breathmaker, show us the man who will lead us in Ceremony."

A high-pitched scream pierced the night sky, causing some men to flinch. A bird of prey. It was spoken.

Broken Tree turned to face the man anointed to usher in the new harvest.

"Red Eagle. Your name has been spoken."

He was stunned. This honor had eluded Red Eagle his entire life. Not after marrying Sapoth. Not after his grandfather, the chief, had died. Emotion filled his arms and legs and chest. He had given up hope, but now something rustled within him. Something deeper than ceremony. Something personal.

Menawa handed Red Eagle a pair of rattlers. Feeling their weight in his hand, Red Eagle looked up to catch a glance of Josiah staring at him as he let out his seventh breath of tobacco.

Was that jealousy in the corner of his eye? Red Eagle thought. Before he could consider, men pushed Red Eagle back down the footpath to the Square.

This was no ordinary stroll, however. Something had awakened in him. Each step flashed him through a different moment in his life. Playing here as a child. Stepping into the Square, and getting punished immediately. The look of his mother when he first stomped down the path. Wanting to cry on this march after his grandfather died, but feeling numb with isolation. Marrying Sapoth, the first real love he felt from a Muscogee since his mother's death. It made him feel whole. That thing crawling through his body felt even stronger.

Before he knew it, Red Eagle emerged in front of the Square. With nightfall, only the Sacred Fire lit the Square. It made for a dramatic moment as the snake of men continued their path from the riverside. A line of shadows licked by the spitting flames of a new year's fire. Recognition of his face at the front caused a stir of whispers in every direction. They were just as surprised as he was. He couldn't see Sapoth, but he looked for her.

His grandfather, the great chief, had led this exact ritual

many times. Red Eagle closed his eyes, and breathed in the memory of the old man's song. It was his favorite Muscogee song.

The men had stopped at the edge of the Square. Red Eagle was left alone to step around the Sacred Fire. He kept his rattlers still, and the scene descended into utter silence. It was time to begin.

A soft sound crawled from his throat. "Who is worthy of the fire?" he asked.

He thought he heard feet shuffling among the townsfolk. He paused. Silence. He closed his eyes and took a deep breath. Then, his voice boomed.

"Breathmaker, who among us is worthy of the fire?"

Red Eagle turned his head to the sky and opened his eyes. Would no one join him in this dance?

No matter. He could feel his grandfather's song rise. Slowly, the great rattler shook awake in Red Eagle's hands, and the song found his throat.

"The fire is cold!" Rat-a-tat-rat. Rat. Rat.

"The days are done!" Rat-a-tat-rat. Rat. Rat.

"We are the dust that is left in the dirt." Tat-tat-tat-rat. Rat. Rat.

"You, among the green corn flower, take us home." Rat. Rat.

He let the rhythm pause. Then he gave a rat. Rat. Rat.

This time when Red Eagle shouted, a second voice joined him. "The fire is cold!"

Rat-a-tat-rat. Rat. Rat.

Several more joined in. "The days are done!"

Rat-a-tat-rat. Rat. Rat.

Then, as if Thunder itself was singing, the entire town took over in unison. Red Eagle shook his great turtle-shell rattle over his head, and spun in circles. As if his rattlers had cast a spell on them, the drums joined, perfectly on beat. The voices followed him to the next verse, and to the next.

He threw his voice high and then scooped it low, just as the song played in his head. He swung the great rattle from his shoulder like a battle ax and kicked himself high into the air. A warrior's dance.

He landed with the soft bounce of a predator on the hunt and looked up. Sapoth was standing right in front of him.

Her ribbons still flailing, she had strapped leather stockings to each leg. Box turtle rattles hung from strings on each side. Swinging her legs to the beat, her rattles stirred the sound of a storm in the summer sky.

Answering her call, Red Eagle built his song to a crescendo with a master's precision. He danced wild, each movement a dedication to his grandfather and his mother, a stake in his claim to this tribe. Sapoth's rattles crashed around him, surrounding him with harmonious support.

He asked the Breathmaker for forgiveness and absolution through his verse. He asked for help from every direction, for blessings and gifts, for food and knowledge. He asked for acceptance.

Upon his last verse, he opened his eyes to see the village dancing in a fury around him. With him, against him, all at once. All of them in one motion. The Sacred Fire had claimed them all.

Red Eagle turned to Sapoth and ripped a ribbon from her tunic. An unburnt prayer is never answered. He threw it into the fire, the ribbon igniting instantly with an orange glow. He spun around and seized another as Sapoth continued to swing her hips.

As Red Eagle snatched the last of his wife's ribbons, the women appeared with the final ashes from last year's fire, tossing it onto the blaze with a quick poof of light. Offerings of pots and clothing were thrown in the Sacred Fire. Each piece of fuel that thanked the Breathmaker for keeping the fire lit all this time would keep them warm, fed, and alive for another year.

Between a gap in the raging flames, Red Eagle spotted Broken Tree. He stood at the edge, staring into the fire. Flames filled his eyes, which never drifted from the blaze until the fire finally retreated toward the coals. Broken Tree looked to Red Eagle, pride in his eyes. It was time to close the ceremony.

Piercing through the reverie with a warrior's scream, Red Eagle, his moccasins wrapped snugly on his feet, jumped into the ring of fire. He danced in the coals, kicking them with ash and stamping them into the ground. He danced with a fervor that froze everyone else in their tracks. He was lost in a trance, and when he punctuated the dance with one final stomp, he was greeted with silence.

Four young women each brought large branches to the fire pit and laid them in separate directions that crossed in the center. His old bones moving carefully, Broken Tree crouched and dropped kindling to the ground from his pocket. He rubbed a small stick between his hands when Josiah appeared beside him, leaning over to pour a fragrant oil from a small pouch. Flames licked the kindling, and climbed the branches.

The fire of the new harvest had arrived. The new year was here.

The Muskogee let out a jubilant cheer. At long last, it was time to feast. A rush of bodies headed for the food, but Red Eagle had eyes only for his son who rested in Onawa's arms. He floated straight for her.

"You should always be proud of your father," she told the baby, and handed him back to Red Eagle.

Sapoth arrived by their side, and the three embraced beside the warmth of the growing fire. He kissed her as deeply as he ever had. The dance had awoken something in him. Something he had forgotten.

With a chatter of soft yip-yip-yips, a large cup of White Drink arrived. The black mixture of roots and herbs sloshed over the side as the first man took a deep sip.

Red Eagle turned his son so he could see.

"White Drink purifies the soul."

Red Eagle placed his son on Sapoth's shoulder and greeted the cup with both hands. He sipped deeply of the foul concoction, but did not swallow.

After every man on the Square had sipped, in one giant motion, they spat the White Drink from their mouths. The long thin streams of dark liquid arced above their heads and crashed down into the earth below in a white foam.

Josiah did not spit his White Drink. He swallowed it in one gulp, and reached back for the cup and downed the remains.

Red Eagle rushed to him. "What are you doing, brother?"

Josiah waved him away. The medicine man fell to his

knees, clutching his stomach. Red Eagle put a hand to his shoulder but it was pushed away.

Broken Tree stood behind him.

"Let him be."

Red Eagle held his elder's eyes for a moment, nodded, and returned to his family as Josiah vomited into the earth. A second wave of vomiting was even more violent, and it got worse with each wave, until at last he rolled onto his side, his face white, and he closed his eyes.

Dawn had arrived. The celebration was over. The rising sun revealed a sparse Square Ground. It was all the permission they needed to head home, and the Muskogee stumbled back to their beds. Red Eagle looked for Sapoth. She grinned through tired eyes.

It was time to ride home.

CHAPTER 3

The Man in the Mansion

The rumble of hooves outside Red Eagle's home shook him from his serenity. He walked straight to the window, but was relieved to see it was only his horses galloping across the paddock. That relief concerned him. A trader should welcome the arrival of strangers, and this anxiety was new. The horses were running together in a pack. At least they looked happy, he thought.

The last trader, an American, had given him a newspaper, now dated three weeks old. Though he had new stock to shelve, he had fallen behind this morning. It was the newspaper stories that distracted him.

"Upper Creek Indian Troubles Grow," the headline read. Violence erupted between white men and natives to the north. Squabbles over minor debts, like the one he owed McKee, had erupted into skirmishes. Perhaps they were more substantial debts, he hoped, but then again, Europeans were not known for respecting the natives.

The newspaper horror stories, which Red Eagle took with a grain of salt, claimed that when the Europeans' debts were not collected, they took land instead. He had always heard these stories from the native peoples, and they concerned him, but he had also known hundreds of Europeans in his life, if not more, and none had treated him that way. That these stories were also appearing in the American newspaper was troubling indeed. It was all he could hope that staying an honest man would keep danger at bay, but with the price of furs falling, the tribes had less to trade with the Europeans, and less with Red Eagle as well. He hated owing anything to anyone, and couldn't wait to get out of this McKee debt. Still, it was virtually impossible to shake the sense that trouble was coming.

A second rumble of hooves shook his windows. This was much bigger. These were not his horses out to play. Setting the paper down, he calmed his nerves. He eyed his musket behind the counter. It was loaded. Ammunition and gun powder were at the ready. He would do what he always did, and use coffee to bait them into entering his shop, putting them at ease, and him in control. He cautiously stepped for the door.

Directly in front of his home, eight horses came to a halt. On their backs sat men in blue military uniforms. Swords hung at each of their sides. Red Eagle emerged into the sunlight to see them in all their splendor, and he didn't feel good about it. He should have brought the musket with him, after all. They better like coffee, he thought.

The man in front wore a jacket finer than all the rest. His collar was the stiffest, his cuffs the whitest, his buttons more numerous and as bright as the sun. It was as if the rest of the men spent all their time making him look good. His face was worn, and oval. His eyes were hooded and did not inspire trust. An officer to his right had a head full of fiery red hair.

"Are you William Weatherford?" the officer said.

"Yes, sir. I'm Weatherford."

"Good," interjected the man in the front, swinging from the stirrup and landing neatly in front of Red Eagle. He passed his reins to the rider with the red hair. "I'm Governor Claiborne. I've come for you."

Red Eagle had never met the governor, nor had he ever had any dealings with any intermediaries of the Alabama Territory at all. It was a suspicious thing to hear, that was certain. He was filled with a feeling of dread. A guest was still a guest, however, and a good trader always offered hospitality.

"Coffee?" he asked, leading the governor inside.

"Capital idea."

While Red Eagle went to the stove, Claiborne prowled the perimeter of the room, looking at the goods piled up on the trading post's shelves. Watching from the corner of his eye, Red Eagle saw the governor pause to sniff at bags of herbs and tea, then to feel the fur on rabbit pelts. Seeing the small selection of books in one corner, he gave a surprised smile.

"Tacitus, Shakespeare, and Saint Augustine. You are well read for a frontier man, Mister Weatherford."

"My father's doing," Red Eagle replied.

"It's an eclectic selection."

Red Eagle shrugged. "I can't say I have much choice in what I can get hold of, only that I read what I obtain."

"And what's this?" Claiborne fingered a row of bone and feather charms hanging from a shelf.

"Made by one of the Creek medicine men," Red Eagle said. "For protection."

Claiborne snorted but said no more.

Having poured two cups of steaming coffee from the pot on the stove, Red Eagle gestured to a pair of chairs beside the counter.

"Thank you," the governor took his coffee and sat down. "I suppose you want to know why I'm here."

"It has crossed my mind," Red Eagle watched his guest with steady eyes that concealed his wary spirit.

"We've heard rumors of a cargo of contraband being moved up from the Gulf. Guns, mostly, from the Spanish, intended to stir up more trouble with Muscogee around here," the governor said, his gaze equally steady. "You haven't seen or heard of anything about that, have you?"

"Can't say that I have," Red Eagle said.

"You wouldn't mind if I have a look around your place to confirm that, would you?"

"I would be happy to show you the storeroom," he replied. The men locked eyes. "Or beneath the house, whatever you need."

"I don't think that will be necessary. But can I count on your help?"

"Help?"

"Help with the Indians." Claiborne sipped his coffee. His mouth curled at the corners, but he gave a satisfied smack of the lips. "You've heard about the troubles up north?"

"Just read it in the newspaper."

"You got your hands on a newspaper?"

"An American passing through gave it to me. It's a few weeks old, so I may not have the latest, but yes."

"Of course. The well-read frontiersman. As you may

know, an uprising of the natives by the Great Lakes is stirring. We believe the British are behind it. Bastards are still sore from losing the war, trying to use savages to sabotage our nation. Working with a redskin fellow by the name of Tecumseh. He's raised a revolt against our government, unleashing violence, forcing peaceful tribes to the brink of war."

Red Eagle frowned. He'd heard whispers of this Tecumseh, but as a political leader, not some sort of bandit bringing chaos and death. Funny how each side told a story that was convenient to their own needs. He wondered what the truth was.

"I've heard of him," he said. "But as you say, he lives way up by the Great Lakes."

"He did, but he's on the move. Heading down here to rally more redskins to his cause. Rumor is the Spanish are stoking the flames along with the Brits. I'll be honest with you, Mister Weatherford, that has me…" he paused to take a sip, before making a satisfied noise and continuing, "worried. It should worry you, too. Our lives down here depend on peace. Like your trading post, my governorship relies on friendly interchange between people."

Red Eagle groaned inside. Friendly interchange would be nice, but even his Scottish father taught him that most frontiersmen didn't come to this territory as friends. They were refugees and opportunists, wearing every color of desperation. He wondered if the newspapers sold lies on purpose, and what harm it did to the people who believed them.

"If Tecumseh stirs up war, everyone loses, not just the folks who follow him. I fear the Creek might join his war."

He sat back, staring into his cup of coffee before picking

it up to take a drink. Red Eagle's thoughts, however, were his own. He recognized the reasonable side of what Claiborne said, but wouldn't be swayed by such a one-sided account.

Growing impatient, the governor exhaled, and stirred his coffee.

"I think you could help maintain that peace," he said. "I can see by looking that you're one of us, but I know you got a little red in you. They respect you over there. That influence is extremely helpful. You sign up with the United States government, and the tribes will think twice before joining up with Tecumseh."

The governor stopped stirring his coffee and tried to coax a glance from Red Eagle's eyes.

"A man of your reputation behind a rifle would be a great asset if war comes 'round."

Red Eagle reached over and set his cup on the counter. He looked down at his hands rather than at the governor as he considered how to express himself. He'd heard good things about Claiborne from people he traded with, but every word the governor spoke made him like him less. This was a man with an agenda. He was just as obsessed with dividing the two sides as Josiah was. The difference was that Josiah saw them from the side of ordinary people living in the woods, and Claiborne saw them from inside the Governor's mansion.

"I'm a trader, Governor Claiborne," he said at last. "I want no part in fighting. I pray that I never have to. Not on either side."

"Then help me avoid it. Stop these damn Indians from stirring trouble."

"My mother was one of those 'damn Indians'. So is my brother. So is my wife."

Red Eagle stood, reached out and took the half-full coffee cup from the governor's hand.

"And my father was a Scotsman and an officer in the Revolution with Washington," he said. "I don't take sides, I take goods, and I exchange them in peace and harmony. If it pleases you, I'm just going to stay here and trade."

"There are two sorts of men in this nation," Claiborne jerked to his feet. The two men stood, their faces inches apart, the governor glaring while Red Eagle kept his calm. "Those who are with the United States and those who are against us. Which are you, Weatherford?"

"Life, liberty, and the pursuit of happiness," Red Eagle turned his back on the governor to set the cup down, and stepped around behind the counter. "I don't remember reading anything in the Constitution about picking fights. I'll help those soldiers feed their families, though."

With his hands hidden, he felt around the cash box for his musket that pointed directly at the table where he just sat. He couldn't fight off eight men, but if there was trouble maybe the threat would be enough.

"I will not fight. Not for you, not against you."

His finger found the trigger.

"If you had a brain inside that half-breed head," Claiborne snarled, "you'd pick a side before someone picks it for you. War is coming, Mister Weatherford."

He stormed out of the trading post and Red Eagle took his finger off the trigger, grabbing the gun and concealing it as he walked to the open door. Claiborne said something low that Red Eagle couldn't hear. His men looked from his nasty expression to Red Eagle, and all eight pairs of eyes glared at him before they turned their horses to gallop away. The ugly barbarian in the red hair kept his hateful gaze on him long after the others. He was the last to leave, and spit on the ground before he did.

"Is everything all right?" Sapoth asked, rubbing the sleep from her eyes as she emerged from the back room. "Sounded like someone was angry."

A cold breeze barked in the door, sending Sapoth searching for cover. Red Eagle shut the door.

"Everything is fine." Red Eagle wrapped his arms around her, enjoying the reassuring warmth of her body. "Everything will be fine."

He only wished that he believed it.

CHAPTER 4

The Way of Peace

The trading post bustled with life. Muscogee Creek from the North rubbed shoulders with Creek from the South, with American settlers, and with other tribes in between. This was not Claiborne's vision for Alabama, it was Alabama in real life. Its people were as varied as the goods heaped around them. Trappers and traders alike leaned against piles of leather britches and bales of tobacco. Parents plopped their little ones on bags of dry goods.

Sapoth weaved between them all, pouring coffee from the pots she kept brewing on the stove. She had a rotation: brew one kettle, pour the other, return, start a new batch, and pour some more. She made this trading post a home, and everyone was better for it. At the door, Red Eagle welcomed guests as they emerged from the last of the dusk. He greeted them with firm handshakes and warm words. Every name and every face was familiar, both sides of his family in the same room. The thought stressed him, having them all in his house simultaneously. But with Sapoth behind him, he felt capable. Everyone had shown their trust in him by coming here in the first place, and they rewarded him with smiles at the entrance.

After the last guest arrived in the deep blue of falling light, Red Eagle closed the door on the cold wind and the stars in the distance. Inside were a warm fire, a well-lit room, and everyone he loved. Navigating through the crowd, he deflected any attempts at small talk, and he knew precisely the impatient ones would ask why he had called them there. They would hear soon enough.

Sapoth placed a steaming cup in his hands, wrapping her fingers around his as she did so.

"I'm proud of you." She looked up at him with a soft smile and those deep brown eyes. He wished he could stare into them forever. "Most men would have given in to Claiborne or kept their heads down and hoped this would blow over."

"Most men are short-sighted. This will not blow over."

He looked over at Josiah, who was scowling at the pale-skinned men from a corner of the room. Nothing could blow over while men felt the way his brother did. Not unless they let go of their anger.

With one swift, fluid movement, Red Eagle leaped onto the counter and turned to face the suddenly silent room. All eyes were trained on him. Part of him was surprised he was even here. Silence came more naturally to him than grandstanding. But as Sapoth had said, he was not a man to keep his head down when trouble knocked on his door.

Red Eagle was a man to stand for what was right.

"Thank you all for coming," he said.

"Thanks for the coffee, cousin," William McIntosh, a medium-skinned man wearing European clothing, called out from the back of the room, raising his cup in salute. A grin split his face from one jet black mutton chop to the other. "Glad to see you don't take after your Scottish relations where hospitality's concerned."

Some of the white folks laughed along with the Muscogee, while others rolled their eyes at the interruption.

"McIntosh, we missed you at the Puskita last week," Josiah lashed. His cold stare was felt across the room.

"Tribal affairs down south kept me away, Josiah." McIntosh was uncomfortable with the insinuation of dishonor. "I trust you spat out a little extra White Drink on my behalf?"

Josiah spat on the floor. Red Eagle stomped his foot on the counter, re-commanding attention.

"As some of you have heard, I shared coffee with another guest two days back," Red Eagle said. "Governor Claiborne."

Whispers ran around the room, some excited, others suspicious. Claiborne had plenty of friends among the white folks but had done little to befriend any native peoples. His name had become a watchword in some parts for white favoritism.

"The governor came to talk with me about Tecumseh," Red Eagle continued. A quiet murmur moved through the room. "You've all heard of him and of what has been happening by the Great Lakes. What you've heard depends upon whom you heard it from. I have a face that allows me to hear from both sides.

"Tecumseh's revolution is coming this way. Claiborne knows it, and he is preparing to stand against it. He demanded that I join him. He was not polite."

The reactions were louder this time, almost everyone turning to their neighbors, wanting to express their feelings at some aspect of this turn of events. Only Josiah and Sapoth stood silent—he with arms folded in front of him, studying the crowd, she looking at Red Eagle, calm and expectant.

Banging his foot on the counter, Red Eagle brought silence to the room once more.

"This land has known peace for many generations. We are a peaceful people, but in moments of weakness, even we will fight. Pride will convince you to pick a side, but do not feed it.

"I look around this room and I see faces of all colors, but I don't see you as one side or the other. I see people I know and love, but mostly, I see myself. As many of you know, my father was Scottish, my mother Creek. I am living proof that we can exist together in harmony.

"Every day, I thank the Breathmaker and God in Heaven for blessing this place where our people join. I will not fight for any cause, white or native, which threatens that.

"If we stand together, we can refuse the call to fight. We can resist being torn apart. Whoever calls you to war, I ask you to tell them what I told Claiborne: I want no part of this fight. I will take no side, and I ask you to do the same."

Applause filled the room, and Red Eagle raised his hand to signal for quiet once again.

"I will condemn no man who chooses to fight for his kin, but I hope that you will stand with me in peace."

Amid further applause, he stepped down from the counter. By the time he landed, he was greeted by enthusiastic guests. The cold wind was a distant memory to the embrace of this warmth.

"Most talking I've seen you do in one go," McIntosh said.

"Hell, it's more talking than I've seen you do in a whole year."

"I only speak," Red Eagle said, "when absolutely necessary."

"Well, allow me, friend," McIntosh replied. "When the time comes, do you really think any of us can avoid getting sucked into this mess?"

"I do," Red Eagle replied.

"I'm not so sure," McIntosh's sturdy frame swayed as he shifted from foot to foot. "The Upper Creek seem to be itching for a fight. I want no part of it. Me and my people in the south like our trade with the white folk too much to mess it up. Hell, in the Lower Creek we actually like the Americans. This ain't our fight. We'd rather be friends with the Americans than the British or Spanish."

As the cards fell on the table and a relaxed discourse filled the room, happiness filled Red Eagle. This was much better than the anxiety he felt after Claiborne's visit. Here, surrounded by family, his wife at his side, and his baby son sleeping in the next room, friends, neighbors, cousins, and laughter filled his home and his heart.

Someone started singing and McIntosh beat time with a wooden spoon against a barrel. The seating was cleared away and dancing quickly followed. White folks and Creek folks traded each other's dances. Beer and whiskey found their way into former coffee cups. Even Josiah cracked a smile.

"You have been lucky in life," Josiah stood beside Red Eagle in a quiet corner of the room, cup in hand. "Between the money your father left and our mother's blood, you have the best of both worlds."

However hard he forced a smile, Josiah could never hide

the jealousy these moments drew out of him.

"I would share it all with you," Red Eagle said.

"No. I have only ever had what the Corn Mother gives me. I do not want the gifts of the white man's world."

"Guess you better give me back that whiskey then," Red Eagle smiled.

Josiah stared for a long moment at his cup.

"If war comes, perhaps it will not be all bad. The spirits have spoken to me. They say that a time of balancing will come. A chance for my people to reclaim what they have lost."

"Our people," Red Eagle said.

"Perhaps." Josiah walked away, leaving his cup behind, but taking Red Eagle's gaze with him.

Sapoth crossed the room and laid a hand on Red Eagle's shoulder. It was a touch that chased away all his cares, and brought him back into the room. Men like Josiah be damned, he wouldn't let anger blind him from feeling joy and camaraderie.

Red Eagle pulled Sapoth close.

"Does it get any better?" he asked.

"Every day," she replied.

In his heart, he felt a light shining bright and full.

In the corner, darkness took over Josiah's face.

CHAPTER 5

Predators and Prey

Red Eagle gazed toward the dawn horizon, waiting for the great sun to emerge. When a gentle light flashed across the horizon, he knew the day was written to be a memorable one. Other days, the dreary days, or the mornings that punish you with heat before the sun even peeks out, meant certain trouble. But this morning was purple in anticipation and gave way to the calm of birdsong. Red Eagle couldn't help but think of his mother in moments like these. Her people spoke the language of the lands, and these were the voices of gentle joy. A gust of wind blew gold across the silvery-blue river. The birds sang back.

"Damn racket," William McIntosh muttered, clutching his head. "What's any creature got to be so cheerful about when it's up at this hour?"

Red Eagle smiled and shook his head. The birds didn't make McIntosh drink so much the night before. Only folks who lived in cities wasted daylight by sleeping past its start. Out here, daylight was worth too much, especially on a hunt day.

For Red Eagle, hunting was never a challenge. Unless it

was a day like this, when McIntosh was sweaty and panting from a night of drink. He stepped on twigs right and left, and vomited right as Red Eagle targeted a deer. He'd never seen a deer move so fast. Time and time again, Red Eagle quieted his mind. McIntosh's pounded, overheating, weak, merciless. There was something to be said for a mixed-race Muscogee raised in a fancy house in Savannah, and it was something Red Eagle liked to remind McIntosh of often. The birds sounded like they were laughing at them.

Crouching in the dew-dappled grass, Red Eagle spotted a patch of trampled plants. There were droppings here. He held his hand over them and felt warmth. Deer were nearby.

A few more moments contemplating the scene revealed that the grass was further trampled off to the right. He looked at McIntosh, who kept his gaze. One look from his eyes and he knew: his cousin was finally awake. Exchanging nods, both slid their muskets off their shoulders, and crept forward.

Rounding a bend in the woods, they spotted a clearing. The grass was long, a hidden treasure that kept the deer focused on feeding, chewing slowly and contemplatively. It was a beautiful morning.

Crouching toward the undergrowth, he found a firing position, his knee supporting his elbow. Careful not to make a sound, he pulled back the hammer, opened his powder horn and primed the pan. Beside him, McIntosh did the same.

Upon their ready, Red Eagle gave McIntosh a slow nod. It was customary that the man who brought home the least game on their last hunt got first shot. The range was long but the air still. *It could be fairly difficult*, Red Eagle thought, *with a hangover.*

The deer's ears perked up. It raised its head and jerked it back and forth. What startled it wasn't them, but that didn't matter now. If they were going to kill the deer, this was the time.

A sharp crack and a cloud of smoke announced McIntosh's shot. Splinters burst from a tree beyond the deer.

The creature bolted, bounding across the clearing, away from them and toward the right.

Following the deer's path with his musket, Red Eagle let out a long breath and then squeezed the trigger.

The bang was loud beside his ear and smoke tickled his nose.

The deer reared up, then fell dead in the grass. Birds scattered into the air.

"You put extra powder in that shot," McIntosh shook his head. "I felt that one in my head. Least I don't have to carry a deer."

"I wonder what spooked it," Red Eagle looked around for other signs of movement.

"Could be anything." McIntosh walked toward the clearing. "Could be it smelled my manly presence. Could be the clacking of those damn beads in your hair. Whatever it is, less dawdling and more walking. I ain't gonna catch up while we're standing around like this."

∼

The long walk back to the trading post wasn't easy, at least for Red Eagle, not with the animal on his back. Fortunately, he wasn't alone with his thoughts. He wasn't alone at all, not since McIntosh's hangover passed and his cousin crawled out of its shadow. It helped to hear McIntosh laugh at his own jokes, or to tell stories to take Red Eagle's mind off of the meat he was carrying. This was why he hunted with McIntosh so much. The man could really ramble, and ramble he did, sharing the gossip from the community—which trade deals were being made, which farmer was milking his maid while his wife visited her sick sister. It wasn't pleasant conversation, but it took Red Eagle's mind off the burn in his shoulders and his back. Step after step, story after story, he was focused on listening about Thomas from the North whose mother was a drunk. Their laughter filled the forest alongside birdsong.

As they approached the edge of the woods, the tone of the songs changed. The trilling of songbirds was replaced by the croak of carrion. A smell of burning drifted through the trees.

Something was wrong.

Hanging their trophies over the branch of a large tree, they reloaded their muskets in tense silence. Side by side, they crept toward the edge of the woods.

As the trees thinned, windows of flame became visible through the foliage. Black smoke billowed up into the blue sky. Fear clutched at Red Eagle's heart. Palms sweating, he tightened his grip on the musket with urgency in his trigger. He frantically scanned the scene for a threat.

One glance across the pasture and, two hundred yards away, the truth was burning. Fire engulfed Red Eagle's entire home. Timbers were blackened and disintegrating. A single flaming curtain flapped from an upper window, then was snatched by the wind and spiraled down to the ground. With a crash, the roof gave way, sparks flying and drifting upward in a cloud of smoke. The horses, trapped in their pasture, ran to the far end where they whinnied and hooved at the ground, wide-eyed with terror.

Red Eagle watched as his home and business fell into blackened ruin, but it was fear for his family that pounded his heart like a war drum. Somehow, Red Eagle kept himself under control. Looking all around for signs of attackers, he stalked out of the woods, careful to avoid an ambush, gun raised and ready.

Beside him, McIntosh let out a low, angry growl.

"What monster did this?" he asked.

"Could be an accident." Red Eagle didn't believe it, but it was one possible truth.

A young man in dirty farmhand's clothes ran around the corner and up the road in front of them. Red Eagle jumped out and grabbed the man by the shoulders.

"Jeremiah, it's me. What have you seen?"

The farmhand was shaken, his eyes wide. "Militia. Twenty of them. Rode up and demanded to search the house." He caught his breath. "Your wife wouldn't let them in without you there. They broke a window and she fired a warning shot…"

Red Eagle let go of his shoulder and ran down the road to the smoking remnants of the house.

Red Eagle had turned away the War, but then it came to his door.

Squatting to peer more closely at a fence post, Red Eagle saw threads of blue material caught in the splintered remains. *Claiborne.*

Dread clutched Red Eagle's heart and ripped it downward with an icy tug.

McIntosh burst past Red Eagle for the paddock beyond the house.

Red Eagle rose and stalked toward him, caution cast aside as the stricken expression on his friend's face sent a spike of terror deep into him. McIntosh turned as he approached and held up a hand.

"You don't need to see," the big man tried to hold him back. "Don't come any closer."

Brushing him aside, Red Eagle stepped past the end of the building and looked into the field.

Sapoth lay there, her hair tangled around her head, one of her beautiful eyes no more than a socket full of blood. Her clothes were torn and muddy, her skirt twisted around her waist, her beauty battered and cast aside.

Red Eagle's heart fell into an abyss. For a moment, the world did not exist.

Then he noticed something by her side, and it pulled him back into the life around him.

His son, once the sweetest innocence, lay still and pale. His perfect, soft face was a dark, disturbing blue. He would never have a name.

Red Eagle fell to his knees beside them and felt his heart scream. The warmth of love that filled his soul had vanished. There was a hole in his spirit, and tears flooded from him. He reached for them, begging for a heartbeat. Nothing was left but despair.

He pulled Sapoth into his lap. He put his hand behind her head to cradle her. Instead of the smoothness of her hair, he felt the ruin of shattered bone and pulped flesh.

The voice of someone screaming, terrible and relentless, disturbed him.

Eventually, he realized, it was him.

A horse galloped across the field. McIntosh rode it bareback out of the gate, the other terrified beasts following in his wake, scattering away from the fire.

"Gonna find those bastards," McIntosh yelled as he rode.

Red Eagle didn't hear him. He was in another place. There were no birdsongs, there was no light, there was no peace.

His whole world was taken from him. His whole world was dead.

CHAPTER 6

Foreign Agents

A fire flickered in the darkness of the Creek camp. Somewhere among the black shapes of the trees, there was movement. Little Warrior scanned the darkness nearby. Josiah followed his glance.

"Who's there?" he called out.

It took Red Eagle a moment to realize that the words were meant for him. He was too numb to quiet the threat. If death reached him before the firelight, so be it.

"Red Eagle?" Josiah asked, squinting. "I didn't think you would come, you being the man of peace and all…"

As Red Eagle stepped into the firelight, the heavy burden in his arms silenced everyone around the fire. A hundred pairs of eyes turned to Red Eagle.

"Oh, my brother." Josiah rushed forward, reaching to take the weight from Red Eagle's trembling arms. The medicine man looked down at Sapoth and the child. Anger burned in his eyes. "Who did this?"

Red Eagle, eyes red and teary, looked to his older brother. He couldn't say the words. The hurt was too deep. He closed his eyes and was filled with the sound of his house burning, of the imagined wails of his wife and the blood-curdling cry of his baby, defenseless as his mother fought for what was right, but was raped and beat to a bloody, lifeless pulp. He couldn't escape the horror. He opened his eyes again.

"Claiborne."

Stumbling like a drunk, Red Eagle moved for a bench beside the fire. The large clearing was crowded with tents, fires, people, and, now, anguish. There were smiles no more. Darkness had arrived.

His people and his wife's people.

"Bury her in the way of the tribe," Red Eagle said. This was the one thing he had been able to grasp amid the shock and the horror. Sapoth was full-blooded Creek. She would not have wanted her body to lie in a cemetery of the white men who did this to her. "The child too. He should be... He didn't even have a name."

He collapsed onto the ground.

While words failed Red Eagle, the Wind Clan surrounded him with songs of mourning, their voices wobbling with emotion. Men carried away the bodies. Josiah placed an arm around Red Eagle's shoulders, and tears flowed from them both.

∽

The visitors arrived at noon the next day.

Red Eagle hoped that it was all a horrific dream, but it never left. The only feeling that remained was a terrible numbness that never stopped. He sat beside the bodies. They were wrapped and prepared for burial, and he felt his lips move, his voice say prayers that were forever burned into his memory when his mother buried his father. It was as if someone else was coaxing them out of him. Sapoth's family looked to him in their grief, but he couldn't bear facing their eyes, not like this.

The trot of horses took them all out of their haze. New arrivals slowed and descended from their horses in the shadows before emerging from the forest and into camp.

One was native. Not Creek, but with more northerly features. Pawnee perhaps. He carried himself with pride, assured in his own stature and skill.

The other two were whites. They wore the loose tunics and trousers of hunters, but their boots were those of soldiers with pointed toes and well-polished leather beneath a fresh spatter of mud. Both had an air of restraint and respect. The blond man stood more stiffly than his counterpart with the black mustache.

"Tecumseh." Josiah greeted the Pawnee with a reverent tone. "I thought that you would travel by night, to avoid the Americans."

"I am afraid I do not know your lands as you do." For all the warmth Tecumseh's face lacked, he made up for it in his eyes. "Besides, why would three innocent travelers on the road need to avoid Americans?"

"These are the men you spoke of?" Josiah asked, turning eagerly to face the white men.

"This is Señor Cardona, a representative of the Spanish crown." Tecumseh gestured toward the dark-haired man and then toward the blond. "And his British counterpart, Mister Smith. As promised, we have the backing of other powers to combat the Americans."

"Your word is good," Josiah's voice rose for the whole camp to hear.

Many people nodded.

A commotion on the edge of camp announced new arrivals. William McIntosh descended from his horse and addressed Tecumseh.

"Chief William McIntosh of the Lower Creek. With me is Chief Major Ridge, a Cherokee of the Upper Coosa."

Ridge walked into the light wearing European garb, similar to McIntosh.

McIntosh approached Red Eagle, lowered his head to Red Eagle's, and placed his forehead to his cousin's. Both closed their eyes until McIntosh rose to his feet, placing a heavy hand on Red Eagle's shoulder, where it would remain.

"If I may speak more," Tecumseh said.

As Red Eagle sat in silence beside the bodies of his family, a space was cleared in the center of the camp. Everyone but him gathered around, sitting on blankets, logs, or the dirt of the Creek lands. The foreigners sat at the edge of the circle. Tecumseh stood in the center, staring out at the gathered people with dark eyes.

"I will not burden your ears for long. You do not need me to tell you of the darkness we face, the same darkness that threatens my people of the lakes and yours of the creeks. It spreads across our lands as surely as any plague or infestation. The blight of the Americans.

"We lived here long before they arrived, but these white men claim our lands as their own. Our lands give us food, they give us shelter. We take care of our people, but the white men claim that their laws are superior, and they bring poverty, death, and injustice. Our faith is the faith of the first men, who respected the Great Mystery, but the white men claim their religion is better than ours.

"Brothers, the white people are like venomous serpents: when chilled, they are feeble and harmless, but encourage them with warmth and they will poison everything to death."

He looked around the circle, waiting for a response. Some were nodding their agreement, others frowned and muttered under their breath. Most sat in thought, their expressions holding an uncertain course.

McIntosh interrupted the silence first. "We live in peace with the Americans. We share families with them. Trade with them. They are more a part of our lives than the Pawnee, and they have stockpiles of food and guns. I have seen them. If they offer the peace that we all want, what do the British and Spanish among us possibly have to offer?"

Less nodding from the group. Many remained still. Tecumseh watched them all. Through the fog of his own grief, Red Eagle saw a flicker of calculation cross the Pawnee chief's face.

"And others?" Tecumseh said.

"There is wisdom in much of what you say," Broken Tree said. "But there is trouble, too. We have lived at peace with the Americans for many years. Why should we risk that for an outsider who knows not what passes amid the forests and the creeks?"

All eyes found Tecumseh.

"You are right," Tecumseh bowed his head to the elder. "Just as we should not live our lives by the word of the white man, the Creek Nation should not live by the words of the

Pawnee. This is your land. These are your people. I have not lived among you, but I know you are not fools. Even the blind can see that the Americans are destroying all we hold dear. If you have not come across a deer or beaver, skinned for its hide, its meat left to rot in the sun, perhaps you don't feel it as deeply as do I. Perhaps, you haven't seen it firsthand. But I have, and I've seen hundreds. Trust your own instead."

He looked over at Red Eagle, still sitting beside the shrouded bodies, and the gaze of the Creek people followed his.

"Even in the lakes, the myth of Red Eagle is widely known. A man of two bloods, two minds. The wisdom of two worlds. I am pleased to see him with my own eyes. Red Eagle, greetings. Share your words."

Red Eagle knew that Tecumseh was playing to his pride. The name of 'Red Eagle' may be known in the lakes, but more likely as the man who gave up a chiefdom to live among the whites. Even here, among his own people, Red Eagle was not sure if he commanded respect. He was both an outsider and chief among them. He was the alien and the sage. But none of this changed that the Creek were silent, waiting for his answer. Gossip is the currency of idleness. At war's horizon, nations turn to men of action, men of strength. Perhaps he did command their respect.

In addition to this uncertain attention, he felt a second weight press down upon him. The grief that bore his soul to the ground. Who deserved his attention now? His family or the Creek Nation? He felt the eyes of Josiah. The eyes of McIntosh. He saw the determination in Tecumseh's eyes and the calculation that lay behind it like a face beneath a shroud. This was not a man he would choose as an enemy.

"There will be war," Red Eagle's voice carried around the camp. A terrible certainty descended upon him. "The Americans will make sure of that and then blame us when it happens. If we had fought sooner, we may have fought to an advantageous peace. But if we leave it any longer, all will be lost. The white man's war is inevitable. All we can do is choose to fight while an equal peace might still be ours."

"Wisely spoken," Tecumseh raised his arms as if preparing to make a grand speech.

"War is not an end in itself," Red Eagle continued. All eyes, including Tecumseh's, turned upon him once more as he rose to his feet. "We must show our strength. The Americans must no longer ignore our wishes. Only then can we make a new treaty, one that allows us to live in peace without bowing to their whims.

"We are not strong enough to destroy them. It is possible for all nations to stand at the end. War is not for supremacy but for equal terms in this new world."

All around the camp, men and women nodded their agreement. Tecumseh nodded, not in enthusiasm, but in acceptance. He admired Red Eagle's sway. It was not the total war he came for, but it would work for now.

Tecumseh took a bowl of red paint and turned to Josiah, painting the red circle of war on his forehead. Others circled Tecumseh, ready to take the mark.

McIntosh and Ridge walked back to their horses on the edge of camp and departed.

Lines were drawn.

CHAPTER 7

The Burning Fire

Camp was alive that night. The fire cracked and bristled, and the men burned through tales of wars past, eager to aim their weapons for the Americans. The memories of horrific deeds and bloodied heroes stirred the air electric. To fight was to dance with death in hopes of taking trophies along the way.

In the shadows beneath the trees, Red Eagle sat alone. The silence of night was the worst part. How he longed to tend to his crying son. To hear his first laugh and watch his first steps. To taste Sapoth's kiss, soft and sweet, her lips full with all the answers to the Great Mystery. He wished to smile through Sapoth's soft little lady snore, to try not to wake her with laughter when she passed gas after she fell asleep. It was all he wanted, to once again have his arm pinned beneath Sapoth's head as a pillow.

He wanted his family back. He looked over to the bodies beneath the mourning shrouds. One infant, one adult. He was so tired, he thought he saw the shroud moving by Sapoth's face. Her body moved. A muffled cry for help, she was trapped. He rushed over to her, and fumbled to undo her shroud. He took a knife to her shroud, ripping it open to give her air, only to find her inside, bound, and gagged, eyes wide in strangulation. He tore at the ropes, desperate to free her, and an arm grabbed his wrists.

He had fallen asleep. He was roused to find the fire was still burning at the Creek camp. It was quieter than before, but the oppressive grasp of war still squeezed breath from his throat.

He saw the silhouette of a man standing above him. For a moment, Red Eagle wondered if death had come for him, too. He would not resist if the supernatural offered reunion with Sapoth and their baby boy. A log cracked, and the shuffle of flames revealed the face of Tecumseh.

"She will always visit you in your dreams," Tecumseh said.

"I hope not," replied Red Eagle, sitting up.

"The dreams are still angry, I see. You clawed at the dirt. May I join you?" the Pawnee chief asked.

"These woods are not mine," Red Eagle patted the log on which he sat. "It is not for me to say where you may go."

Tecumseh settled down on the log with a creak. There was a rustle in the bushes as some small creature scampered away.

They sat in silence for a while. Whatever Tecumseh wanted, Red Eagle was not going to ask him about it. If the war leader wanted him to talk, he would have to pry it out of him.

"At the fire, we talked about the war," Tecumseh said at last. "About who will lead the Creek in fighting the white men."

"I am both a Creek and a white man. My world does not divide as neatly as yours."

"You are right. Let me choose better words. We have discussed who will lead the free people in fighting against the

Americans."

Again, silence fell between them. Silence could be many things—a respite for thought, a moment of calm, a sign of comradeship and peace. Tecumseh used it the same way he used his words—as a lever with which to turn men to his will. Red Eagle understood the games men played. It would take more than a lever to move him.

"Your people say that you should lead," Tecumseh said. "You are strong and you are wise. They know you are committed to this war."

"No."

"No, you are not committed? Or no, you will not lead?"

"I accept the inevitability of what is coming. I will not rush to embrace it."

"I am glad you say that," Tecumseh said. "It proves what I have thought since I first walked into this camp."

Red Eagle was unable to resist.

"Which is what?" he asked.

"That you and I are the same. A fire burns within you, a passion that could burn away the world if you were ever to set it free. But you understand that the world is a fragile, precious place.

"Until you spoke tonight, I had forgotten about the importance of restraint in all things. I allowed too much of my fire out. I lost sight of the way this war must end and the way it must be fought. That restraint, that code, is the way we fight. If we do not, we risk burning away the world we mean to save."

The end of the log splintered as Red Eagle's fist tightened around the wood. He did not like Tecumseh's presumption to understand him. Nevertheless, there was truth in what the other man said, and the rage that burned within was as much in that truth as in the presumption.

"If I do not lead then who will?" Red Eagle asked.

"I do not know. Your brother, Josiah, is most eager, but his fanaticism is best unleashed on the battlefield. It is not meant for planning and strategy. If we must do this, we must do it for the right reason. Your reason. I will not poison that."

Just enough light reached through the forest canopy for Red Eagle to make out Tecumseh's face. It could have been a trick of the darkness, a lack of detail that hid the truth, but he did not see the same calculation that had been there before. He saw an honest man, leading others down a terrible but necessary path.

"I do not like this war," Red Eagle said. "It has not yet begun, but it has already taken my life. If the Creek do not fight, they will lose everything, too.

"I am as much a part of the American nation as the Creek nation. But only one nation is threatened by destruction. America will survive. If my Creek brothers want me to lead, if you want me to lead, then it is my duty."

"I do not know if I have done a good or a bad thing here tonight," Tecumseh said. "But I rest more peacefully knowing we will be on the same side."

Together, they stood and walked out of the shadows, heading for a group of men at the edge of the firelight. It was the Creek chiefs speaking in hushed tones with the English and Spanish agents. They all turned as Red Eagle and Tecumseh approached, waiting for an answer.

"If you will it, then I will take your lead," Red Eagle said. "I will command our people against the Americans."

Their smiles of relief showed him that Tecumseh had told the truth—they wanted Red Eagle to lead them.

"We have troops operating all along the northern border," Mister Smith's crisp British accent cut through the chatter of the Creeks. "Until we can join up with you, we'll look at bringing in some guns. Help you chaps give the colonies the sharp kicking they deserve."

"We have guns too," Señor Cardona said. "We can move troops up from Florida. What you take, we will hold."

"Thank you," Red Eagle said. Taking on the United States was too much for the Creek tribes alone. With foreign backing, they might stand a chance.

"What is your plan?" one of the elders asked.

"Send me your finest warriors. Wolves always gather before a hunt."

Galvanized by the orders, the men found their horses and scattered into the distance.

The Creek were hungry for war.

CHAPTER 8

The Eye of the Prophet

Josiah watched as Red Eagle accepted his place as war chief and gave his first command. It was all going exactly according to plan. A leader he trusted. His brother finally choosing his side. The secret ceremonies had worked.

As the elders dispersed, Josiah too turned away. If he could leave his brother to talk with Tecumseh, all the better. Let Red Eagle fix upon this path. Let him learn from the man who had rallied war among the lakes. Together, they could not be defeated.

Unlike the elders, Josiah had no marching orders. Not from Red Eagle, at least. His place was as a warrior on the battlefield, and as a medicine man off it. And, now, finally, his brother was doing as he wished. All there was left for Josiah to do, while the others gathered troops and sent the call to arms, was to prepare himself. He could allow himself the contentment to enjoy his masterwork. It was pride that he felt in this moment.

But there was an itch inside that would not allow him to relax. It was excitement. Later, perhaps, he would rejoin the circle and listen to old war stories, but now, his excitement would be best suited for solitude. He fetched a burning brand from the communal fire and made for his hut to thank the Breathmaker for answering his calls.

Ducking through the doorway, he laid the brand among the kindling in the unlit hearth. Flames swiftly rose through the neatly stacked wood, illuminating his home instantly. Yes, the Breathmaker willed this to be done, and now he must honor that generosity. He scanned his hanging meats toward his arsenal of herbs and plants. He must find the perfect offering, but in the corner, sitting by his weapons, a dark figure sat, facing him. Had he been there the entire time?

"Who are you?" Josiah demanded, raising the brand like a weapon.

"I have many names," the man said. "Some for men and some for beasts. Some for this world and some for the spirits. You may call me Tenskwatawa."

Josiah dropped the brand into the fire and stared in awe at the man before him—Tecumseh's brother was the great spiritual voice of the Red Stick rebels.

"I am honored to receive you in my home," Josiah sat cross-legged on the floor.

"I am honored to be here," Tenskwatawa said.

The great medicine man leaned forward, the fire revealing his face. He had much of the dignity of Tecumseh, but a weariness about him too, as if he had seen far more than other men of his years. A thin mustache decorated his upper lip. His right eyelid was half closed, and the eye beneath it was a dull, milky white.

"Which eye do you think I see farthest with?" Tenskwatawa asked.

"This one," Josiah pointed to the left.

"No." Tenskwatawa pointed to the ruined right eye. "This one is not hampered by the world around us."

Josiah looked at the mystic uncertainly. Tenskwatawa's riddle showed a deep wisdom that both delighted Josiah and made him feel foolish all the same. At least no one else was there to witness.

"Why have you come to me?" Josiah asked. "There are others who might have given a wiser answer."

"True. But no one is born a hunter. We must learn to hunt along the journey. The same is true for wisdom."

Despite the warmth of the hut, he drew his blanket higher around his shoulders.

"Once, I was a drunk and an outcast," Tenskwatawa said. "I have come far to reach wisdom and understanding. Your journey will be shorter, but no less important."

"My journey?" Josiah asked.

The firelight seemed to smolder from inside Tenkwatawa's eyes as he looked at him. "Your journey to become a prophet for your people, and a guide for your brother."

"I am honored."

"Yes, but keeping him on the path laid by the Great Spirit will be no easy task. The Great Spirit. The Breathmaker. These are only names. And there is only one question. Are you worthy?"

Josiah's eyes flicked across the fire. If he was certain of only one thing, it was of his own strength. His will to follow the path to save his people would not be stopped. He'd drag them, burning and screaming, if he had to. "I am," he replied.

"Let us begin."

Tenskwatawa threw fragrant herbs upon the fire and placed more on the rug beside him. Josiah took out a cooking pot and a jug of water. Together they prepared an infusion to commune with the land beyond human memory. The meticulous process would open their minds to each other, and to the world around them, visible and otherwise.

As they worked, Tenskwatawa told Josiah about Tecumseh and the war they were making in the north. He described the crimes of white men and the encroachments of their United States. Such talk was not new to Josiah, but his characterization was. Tenskwatawa spoke not of politics and nations, but of the restlessness of spirits and the poisoning of a land. The truth crystalized to Josiah. This was not just a war for territory or for survival. This was a war for the spirit of the Creek people, and for the soul of the natural world.

"Tell me of your dreams," Tenskwatawa said as they drank their infusion. "In them you have seen the white man, have you not?"

"I have seen him again and again." The drink warmed Josiah's belly and left him with a deep feeling of peace and comfort, even in spite of the horrors they discussed. "Sometimes he appears in peace. Sometimes he attacks. Sometimes he flees from me and my ax."

"You have shared in my dream," Tenskwatawa said. "In your dream, were you alone?"

Josiah thought back. It was hard to remember. The details of dreams, even important dreams, faded with the light of dawn. He took a deep breath, and closed his eyes. Fragments and instincts began to coalesce. His mind opened. Memories from another world flooded back into view. The elixir was working. The dream returned. "There were others there," he said. "Fighting at my side."

"I was among them," Tenskwatawa's eyes were closed and his face was turned up to the peak of the tent. "Before we met, I knew of your dream because I saw you in mine. This is why I sought you out. Through this dream, the Great Spirit showed me that you and I, together, are destined to drive back the white man."

"Yes," Josiah said. The hut had grown bigger than it ever had before. And porous. As if the breeze from outside passed straight through the hide walls. His mind felt as porous as the tent, open to the world around him. The more the memories pieced together, the more vivid his recollection of Tenskwatawa, a brave with an ax emblazoned by righteousness. "You are right. We drove them back together. Slaughtered them with our axes. Made the land our own."

"It was no dream," Tenskwatawa said. "Your place is that of a prophet. We have shared a vision of the future, of the white man being driven back, of the free people ridding our lands of the United States. This is our will."

"Yes!" Josiah gazed into the fire, wondering how he could have been so blind. This wasn't a dream; it was the future. A powerful heat built within him.

In the firelight of the hut, there was only the two of them, but in the darkness lived flashes of a violent and triumphant future.

"Your brother preaches a war of moderation," Tenskwatawa said. "This will start us in our work, but it will never finish it. You must keep him upon the path to drive the white man screaming from our home. This is the path to victory."

"I will not let my brother stop. Victory will be ours, for the spirits and for all the people of the Creek."

"Good," Tenskwatawa rose to his feet. "Tell me now, who are you?"

Josiah rose and stepped forward to embrace his fellow medicine man. "I am the Prophet Josiah."

CHAPTER 9

Progress and Loyalty

Nothing about this was easy. It had been four days since Red Eagle's world caved in, and it was time to bury Sapoth and their nameless son. It was customary to dig the grave by hand, and if the past four days seemed to last forever, digging the grave felt like a hundred years.

With every tired scoop, he thought of her. Each groan from his arm, and he remembered her caress. He pulled and pulled until his shoulder refused, then he switched, and started back up again. This is what she would have wanted, he told himself. He couldn't give up.

He refused to distract himself with thoughts of the war. He wanted to hold onto her forever, to show her spirit how much he loved her. How he longed to tell her that, just one more time. To see the sparkle in her brown eyes, to see her smile. It was her smile he missed the most.

That smile could silence a room. Their last night together, when everyone gathered in their shop, Sapoth filled cups of coffee for relatives with that smile. Wanting to know why they were there, their guests grew impatient. Each time, Sapoth smiled and reassured them they'd learn soon enough.

He spent the evening nervous of what he might say, but when she smiled, a calm washed over him. Though he did all the talking that night, it was Sapoth's words that he remembered most.

"I'm proud of you," she saved her tender smile only for him and the baby.

How he longed to grow old with that smile, to see it carve out wrinkles on her face. Proof of a life well loved. There was nothing it couldn't disarm.

It was not lost on him that the last time Sapoth was with him, Red Eagle clamored for peace. Now he was burying her before launching war.

Accepting war meant picking a side. But it was never so simple as to draw a line between light and darkness, between these men and those. Whatever side he fought for, Red Eagle was a man of the other side as well. There were white men who deserved his loyalty just as much as the Creek people did.

His greatest responsibility now was to lead the Creek. But he had one other responsibility first. And so, with the help of his people, he placed her body in the grave, his son's tiny body next to her. Others covered them with dirt as they watched what he knew would be his final moments with either of them. Each plop of dirt a perfunctory reminder that his was a life left all to himself. Once the funerary rites were complete, and the bodies were underground, he said his farewell.

"Sapoth, you gave me everything I ever wanted in life," he started, his voice breaking. "You gave me a love worth living for. You gave me a family, a son. I promised you I would love you until our dying days. That I would fight for what I believed in, but I never thought it would mean this. Son, you never knew this life. You will never grow up and never fall in love. I beg you both for forgiveness. It's not what I wanted. I wanted peace, and I wanted our family to be happy, but instead, I did not protect you. You were killed because of me. I will never stop until I make that up to you."

He tucked three flower seeds into the dirt above them. A beautiful family of three that would return to the land and would sprout again much later. Through tears, Red Eagle said his final farewell, turned for his horse, and rode away, alone.

He followed an old familiar path through the forests and across the creeks, to a stretch of land just beyond the place he called home. Gone were the memories of home and harmony. He expected to feel longing at the sight of their ruins, to feel sadness. Instead, he felt only rage. It burned hotter and hotter.

He rode through the farms of the more adventurous white men and the more forgiving natives, the Lower Creek. People willing to live alongside each other, to work together, to learn and to trade in respect. It was the life from which Red Eagle had been born, and which he still wanted. A life that Claiborne had ripped away from him. A life that was a lie.

On a small farm at the edge of the woods, he came to a halt amid fields of corn. He fastened his horse to a pen full of pigs. This was the home of his cousin, William McIntosh.

Red Eagle had barely dismounted when the door of the house burst open. McIntosh rushed over and swept him up in a crushing hug. Frightened chickens squawked at the sudden movement, leaving a storm of scattered feathers in their wake.

"Where have you been?" McIntosh asked. "You scared me, vanishing like that."

"I stayed with Sapoth and the boy until they were at rest," Red Eagle said. "It was how she would have wanted it."

"I've been to a lawyer and met with other American contacts. We need to take what happened to the courts. If Claiborne did it…"

"No." Red Eagle shook his head. "Courts are for white men to decide which white men get an advantage over the rest of us."

"What else is there?" McIntosh's brow furrowed. "War?"

"Claiborne is the governor. He is the law. Even if I beat him in court, another will take his place, and he won't be any different. This system doesn't care about the Creek. More families will suffer like mine. Unless the balance changes."

"The balance?" McIntosh's lips went flat. "What balance?"

"Between the people of the creeks and the people of the states," Red Eagle said. "Between native and white."

"Our people have no chance against the Americans. You've seen their weapons. Dream of balance all you want, but it's a folly, a death warrant. You gonna sacrifice yourself to save someone who's already underground?"

Red Eagle looked at the face of his friend and cousin, and found it almost impossible to say what he must.

"What's a life worth," Red Eagle met McIntosh's eyes, "if they can just take it from you?"

He paused.

"Tecumseh's cause is mine now."

"You cannot be serious!" McIntosh's voice boomed, startling the chickens. "He's using you for his own purposes. Just like the Spanish and the British. Them bastards are no different from Claiborne. They want to drive folks out of their homes, same as him. Only difference is the flag they carry."

"I swear to no flag," Red Eagle stated, trying to calm his friend. "I met Tecumseh. He wants to secure the future of our people."

"That's what he told you, huh? What about the future of the people he attacked up by the lakes?"

"I am leading the fight, William. Not him. All we seek is to defend ourselves."

"Oh, really? Will that be the story when a fellow Muscogee burns down my barn, chases away my horses, shoots at me through the trees? A wise man once told me not to choose a side. Said peace was the answer. I believed him. Still do. The Lower Creek will not join your war."

Silence fell across the farmyard. A shutter creaked as McIntosh's wife peered out at them. A glance from McIntosh sent her back inside. A whimper came from the barn, and Red Eagle could not tell if it was the sound of man or beast.

"We have lived peacefully together before," Red Eagle said. "In the future…"

"To hell with your future," McIntosh snapped. "Tecumseh's future. That's no future of mine. It's not the future we've been working toward all these years. Educating our people. Making progress where we can."

"Watch the White Man burn your house to ground and rape your wife. Then tell me of progress," Red Eagle tried to keep the desperation from his voice. "I lost all hope for progress that day."

He stared with iron eyes as his best friend and cousin drew away from him in fear and anger. He could see the conflict in his eyes. He understood his position. Hell, he championed it. But there was no changing his own path, not after what they did to him.

"I don't blame you," McIntosh's face reddened against his black hair. "But I still have hope. And you're forcing me to pick a side or lose everything I've got."

"You're not…"

"Damn right I am," McIntosh interrupted him, folding his arms across his chest. "I won't let the Lower Creek fall prey to the emotions of our hot-headed brothers to the north. We are better than that. We'll throw in our lot with the Americans. Trade loyalty for peace."

"Loyalty." It was Red Eagle's turn to take a step back, pulling himself in the face of McIntosh's wrath. The small space of the farmyard now seemed like a vast chasm opening up before him, swallowing his friendship and leaving his cousin on the other side. "So we will fight," Red Eagle said. "On opposite sides."

"Seems that way." The heat of McIntosh's fury was tempered by a glimmer of doubt as if he was too scared to jump.

Red Eagle felt the same way, but there was no path back to where they had been. Regret was a shifting riverbank upon which nothing could be built.

"And if we face each other in battle?" he asked.

"I don't know," McIntosh threw his hands up in the air. "I don't aim to shoot you, it that's what you mean. You're… We're…" He shook his head. "Couldn't do that."

"War won't change us," Red Eagle said.

He wanted to believe that. He wanted to close the gap between them, to embrace his friend for what might be the last time. He wanted some memory of what they had been to remain.

"This is not how it was meant to be."

"No," McIntosh said. "But it is what it is."

„I pray you never know betrayal."

Red Eagle turned and mounted his horse. There were no more words. Their paths were clear. Perhaps one day, fate would bring them back together.

He rode away in silence, refusing to look back. All he heard was a door closing behind him and the fading thread of conversation from inside the house. Then it was washed away by the murmur of the wind and the twitter of birds.

Step by plodding step, he rode through the woods and across the creeks. That was enough sorrow for the day.

It was time for war.

CHAPTER 10

The Dead Man in the Blue Jacket

The snap of a twig bolted Red Eagle's eyes open, and he slid his blanket off to the side. Around him, fifty brave warriors lay scattered across the ground of a clearing beside Burnt Corn Creek, sleeping after a long day's hike. Sentries stood at the edge of the camp, peering into the night-shrouded woods. No one else had been disturbed by the noise. For a moment, Red Eagle wondered if it was his imagination; or perhaps the Breathmaker was calling to him.

Then, he heard it again, the unmistakable crack of a stick broken underfoot, somewhere to his left.

With hunter's instincts, he reached for his musket, moving slow and silent. It could be an animal, or one of his men relieving himself in the woods, but Red Eagle couldn't take that chance. Not with Claiborne's troops on the march.

He eased himself onto his knee, raising the rifle with one hand while he reached for his nearest sleeping comrade with the other.

"Now!" someone shouted.

The sound of boots ran out of the woods and along the bank of the creek. The loud bang of musket fire flashed one after the next.

In an instant, the night was full of shadows shifting in the night, gray shapes visible by the light of the moon.

"Press them hard, boys," the same voice shouted. "Show 'em what happens when you war on Alabama!"

It wasn't the words that made Red Eagle's blood boil. It was the voice. Crisp, clear, and arrogant, it was a voice he would never forget. The voice that threatened him just before his family died. The voice of Governor Claiborne.

All around, the Creek warriors woke in confusion. They reached for their weapons, but those at the edge of camp were already overrun. The governor's militiamen stamped on bodies where they lay and beat them with the butts of their muskets.

Rising to his feet, Red Eagle brought his musket to his shoulder, took aim and fired at the nearest shadow. A militiaman cursed and fell screaming to the dirt.

Too late, Red Eagle spotted a better target. One man, on horseback, swung the edge of his saber above his head. Claiborne. The dead man in the blue jacket.

Red Eagle turned to rally his men, but it was already too late. Frantic and scattered, some darted for cover in the woods, others fled downstream. Supplies meant to see them through long months of raiding lay abandoned by the creek.

Red Eagle could not fight them alone. Even with a perfect reload, he couldn't shoot Claiborne before the others would reach him. He knew when he was outmanned. Vengeance would have to wait. He too ran into the woods.

A few feet into the forest he stopped and looked back. The Americans had pushed his people only as far as the edge of the camp. Now, they had turned their attention to lighting lamps and fires, rummaging through the possessions the Creek warriors left behind. He watched them pick up war axes and wave them around in clumsy mockery. They opened rations of carefully preserved dried meat; they also threw blankets on the fires, sending them leaping into flames. He had never known men so careless, both with possessions and with their own safety. Only fools were so shortsighted, so disrespectful.

He turned and crept deeper into the woods. Within a few feet, the first of his warriors crept back into view, seconds from the clear. Arrogance made the men from Alabama foolish. The retreat from the Creek was now their greatest cover. Silently, he called his men down toward the riverbank behind the trees and bushes. His war band found his side.

"Form a perimeter around the edge of the woods," he said, men crowding in to hear his calm, quiet words. "Two arms' length between you. These are not warriors, but you are. Prepare to fight like it."

Though Claiborne's men dressed like soldiers, Red Eagle's men understood the craft of war. Hunting. Tracking. Stalking. A pack strike. They also had an ally the Americans did not: the heartbeat of the woods. They slipped into darkness.

At the edge of the clearing, Red Eagle watched the Americans. Their laughter and jeering almost drowned out the sound of the creek rushing past to his left. And there, in the center, was his target. Governor Claiborne was about to die. Weapons were raised, fury was loaded.

With a whoop, Red Eagle leaped to his feet and rushed forward. His men followed his example, bursting loudly from the tree line, weapons raised. American faces twisted in shock as Creek muskets barked. A few of the soldiers fell in agony, another in silence as half his skull was ripped from his head.

Rushing at the startled Americans, the Creek warriors created enough noise for an army ten times their size, and it was working. Frightened men in blue jackets stumbled backward, tripping on the blankets and supplies they pillaged moments earlier. A few had the sense to frantically start loading their muskets, but not enough to beat the speed of Red Eagle and his men. The rest clawed the ground in search of hatchets, sabers, anything.

Their whooping froze the Americans and the Muscogee war eyes drove the fear deep into their chests. A brave soldier stood in Red Eagle's path, and thrust his bayonet with desperate gusto. Red Eagle dodged right, spinning around the weapon to jab the butt of his own gun into the side of the man's head with a crack of wood on bone.

The body hit the ground with a thud, Red Eagle already stepping over it toward the next man. For a moment, he wondered how many men might be fighting on the other side. A bullet hissed past, ripping his attention back into the moment. Until there's none, there's enough to kill him.

The clearing was chaos, the two sides battling between the fires, their shadows twisting in the shifting light. In the darkness, everyone was dangerous.

Only one figure stood out among the mess. Still mounted on his horse, refusing to fight like a soldier, Claiborne shouted orders futilely at his men. He waved his saber in great arcs through the air, but he wasn't fighting, he was just trying not to get killed. The coward couldn't even use the sword. He stayed behind his men, all bark and no bite.

Hatred in his heart, Red Eagle made straight for the governor. Fighting like a starving animal broken free from its cage, he tore through every enemy in his way. He smashed his rifle into a man's ribs with a paralyzing crunch, and in one swoop picked up a hatchet from the ground and whipped it around to bury it in the next man's neck. The gargled scream was nothing. All that mattered was Claiborne.

At last, the governor's eyes found Red Eagle in the firelight. Claiborne's eyes widened, and he lowered his saber as if to fight. But he was too frightened to hold his gaze, shifting his eyes around the battle, fear filling his face. When he looked again at Red Eagle, his sneer had vanished, his eyes full of horror.

"Fall back!" he yelled to what remained of his soldiers. "Run while you still can!"

Yanking on the reins, Claiborne turned his horse toward the far end of the clearing. Seeing his moment slipping away, Red Eagle sprang forward, raking his ax across an American face, and in a blink, another man's knee.

The governor jabbed his horse's flanks with his spurs, bolting into the night with Claiborne holding on for his life. Red Eagle was too late.

The soldiers who were left fled with full fright, racing away along the riverbank. Some of the Creek warriors gave chase, either to end them or ensure they didn't regroup. The rest of his men got to work. Half surrounded the perimeter, securing the clearing and checking the fallen to see who might live and who still needed to die. The others damped down the fires that threatened to reach the forest and gathered together scattered supplies. Slowly, the clearing returned to silence until only one American voice remained.

"You dirty animals. You're all gonna die."

Red Eagle recognized him immediately by his hair that burned red even in the shadows of firelight. The man whose hateful eyes sickened him to his core. The last look from the men who returned to burn his home, rape his wife, and kill his baby.

"All your land is ours. Whether today or tomorrow. All that you have will belong to us."

Blood was in his mouth, and he clutched at his ruined leg, but the vileness inside him would fight until its last breath. He recognized Red Eagle approaching him, incensing his anger even further.

"I killed your—"

Before he could finish his sentence, Red Eagle split his skull open with a hatchet. The crack was the last noise the man would ever make. Blood covered his blue jacket.

Red Eagle looked back into the darkness. He missed his shot at Claiborne. He wouldn't miss again.

CHAPTER 11

No Rest

From his hilltop defensive line, Andrew Jackson looked out toward the low, swampy land surrounding New Orleans. Somewhere down there, in the fog and the pre-dawn darkness, waited a British army three times the size of his own. A well-trained and disciplined force that killed halfway around the world. Today, their sights were set on him.

He laid his hand on the barricade. The wood was cut rough and quick, a defensive wall unkind to the touch. Like the trench he stood in, it was a haggard line, but it would work. War was not about perfection. It was about hard graft and a sharp mind amid chaos.

"General Jackson, sir." A young lieutenant appeared at Jackson's shoulder and snapped off a sharp salute. To Jackson's weary eye, he looked barely old enough to be called a man. His blue jacket, once the carefully tended uniform of a local militia, was patched and powder-stained. It barely even fit. Jackson wondered who he had inherited it from. "Report from Colonel Hinds, sir. He says the British canal has fallen in, as expected. They're entirely reduced to an assault by foot."

"And the howitzers from the river," Jackson asked, rubbing his chin.

"Oh, yes sir," the lieutenant's face flushed.

The sky was lifting from black to gray in the east. The fog at the base of the hill was beginning to disperse. Jackson caught a glimpse of movement, a shape shifting in the shadow. The briefest flash of red against a green ground.

"What's your name, soldier?" he asked.

"Harding, sir," the young man replied. "Robert Harding."

"Lieutenant Harding, inform the artillery batteries that the enemy is approaching and to open fire as they see fit. Tell the officers to ignore the river. What matters today is the hill."

"Yes, sir." Harding saluted and sprinted away, the fog ripping open as he rushed through.

"Gentlemen," Jackson called out. "Man your posts. The time has come."

Up and down the line, men emerged from their huddles beneath their blankets, finding the clutch of weapons behind the wood and dirt barricade.

Shrugging off their weariness, the men mounted the parapet in rapid succession. They had no coffee in the trenches, but they did have adrenaline. The hiss of powder poured down barrels and the scrape of ramrods flashed down the line. A roar exploded from the river.

"Ignore that," Jackson called out over the din. "The river is blocked. It is a distraction. Don't give in. Don't fire too quick. Fire smart. We are Americans. God and freedom are on our side."

The fog parted, revealing row upon row of British infantry, their bayonets fixed, their muskets raised. They were striding forward, in unison, toward the American line.

"Hold steady," Jackson called out. "Wait until you see the whites of their eyes."

As the last strands of fog lifted, even more British appeared. Columns of grim faces and red coats moved in concert, their metal features gleaming in the sun. More in this single attack than Jackson had in his whole command.

He looked down his line. Eager to unleash hell, the march seemed to last an eternity. His heart began to thunder. The scent of adrenaline filled the air. He took a deep inhale to savor the moment. No one had panicked. At least, they had a shot.

"Wait for it..." Jackson's mouth was dry, his pulse racing toward what was to come. "FIRE!"

A great wave of American gunfire burst forth. The flash of powder brightened the gloom for an instant as the crack of thunder filled the air, the smoke floating from the defenses like a sulfurous fog. Down the line, cannons boomed and ripped the columns of red-coated men to shreds.

"Reload!" Jackson shouted.

Down the line, his officers echoed his cry.

"FIRE!"

The roar of American muskets halted the British advance, sinking the Reds to the ground, stained and frayed. A direct hit threw a cadre of men into a spin as their legs shattered beneath them. But with each fallen soldier, another Brit stepped up. They advanced closer and closer.

"Fire at will!" Jackson bellowed.

Around him, men raced to reload their guns. The time for strategy had passed. Now was time for speed, for precision. Now, they had to take out the marching red or else they would drown in a sea of scarlet slaughter. Time was running out.

The loud roar of a concerted firing line was now a constant crackle of gunfire, punctuated by the thunder of artillery. Behind the lines, British howitzer shells plowed into the rear of New Orleans's defenses, smashing walls and cratering muddy streets. Still out of range.

In the front, the British kept coming. Jackson needed one more bullseye from the cannons. A boom saw a blast miss its mark. Gunfire continued to bark. Some redcoats fell, but not nearly enough. Another boom from the cannons hit its mark. Bodies were sent flying, and with it, British discipline. It wasn't fear, but a desperate animal instinct for survival. Some Reds made a run for it, pushing their unit ahead of their line in a mad-eyed panic. A man in front, raising his sword with a crazed yell, led the charge against the Americans, but was quickly torn apart in a blaze of close-range fire. The unit was felled, one-by-one, until the officer in the rear crumpled at the base of the wall.

There was something admirable about these soldiers, Jackson had to admit. The bastards didn't run for the woods, they continued their advance even after the wounded were dragged back behind them en masse. That unshakeable resolve might break the lines of New Orleans, if enough of them got close.

A British unit reached the timber wall just down the line from Jackson. Some of the British fired up at the defenders eight feet above them, providing cover as their comrades raised their ladders.

"Ladders!" Jackson yelled as he rushed to the position. "Push back the ladders!"

Men dropped their weapons and gripped the tops of those ladders as they reached the wall. They heaved the ladders back, taking the leading redcoats with them. It was an effective order, but it was a costly one, too. One man who pushed off a ladder was immediately hit, and fell from the wall. Another staggered back and collided with Jackson, blood spraying from the ruin of his jaw.

"Keep firing!" Jackson yelled, rushing down to a point where the wall was lower. The British clearly targeted it as a weak point, and were desperate to clamber up. "Don't let them in!"

A man fell to Jackson's right. An instant later, he was dragged clear and replaced by another soldier. He had good men at the wall. The air was thick with smoke. It scratched the back of Jackson's throat, rasping his voice as he ran down the line barking out orders and encouragement while searching for the next ascent. Push back the ladders, and push back the British advantage.

Panicked shouts came from the east. Heart pounding, Jackson raced over, saber in his hand, ready to hack down his part. A vision flashed into his mind of the British streaming up the ladders and into the city, putting the place to waste. He couldn't let that happen.

His imagination had missed the mark. American bullets, however, had not. Instead of a British breakthrough, he saw redcoats running from the walls, the last survivors of a shattered unit. That panic was an infection that ran straight down the British line. A few men broke away from the assault at first, then a few more, and more still until the whole British force was flooding away from the defenses of New Orleans in retreat.

Jackson raised his sword in victory. A ragged yell announced his triumph.

∼

"General Jackson, sir."

Lieutenant Harding snapped to attention in the doorway of Jackson's tent. Like Jackson, he was still stained from the fight. Jackson grinned and Harding's discipline slipped, the same expression filling his face.

"Have you eaten yet, Lieutenant Harding?" Jackson asked, gesturing at the platter of bread and meat on his desk. "Some men find that battle robs them of their appetite, but for me there is no hungrier work."

Harding hesitated, practically drooling as he eyed the plate.

"Come on, man," Jackson pushed the food across the desk. "Don't make me order you to take sustenance."

Laughing gratefully, Harding approached. He handed a letter to Jackson with one hand, while his other eagerly reached for a slice of beef.

"Messenger arrived just after the British left," he said. "From Washington."

With a swift flick of his letter opener, Jackson revealed his latest orders, his gaze never leaving the young soldier.

"No sooner do I beat one enemy than I'm sent to another." He cast the letter aside and reached for a hunk of bread. "A nation at war never sleeps, eh?"

"No, sir," Harding managed through a mouthful of food.

"Tell me, lieutenant," Jackson peered at his orders. "What do you know about the filthy native men they call the Creek?"

CHAPTER 12

Fort Mims

"Why should we go back to the way things were?" Josiah asked from atop a tree stump. His face was full of fervor, his voice booming larger than his stature. "Why should we accept the white men on our lands? We must drive them from the creeks, from the forests, from what is ours, back to their so-called United States. We must make ourselves free. So the Breathmaker says."

Red Eagle did not interrupt Josiah as he spoke to the warriors gathered in the clearing. It was not his place to decide what they believed, only to lead them in battle.

As the listeners cheered, Josiah stood taller. The clearing filled with the buzz of excitement, and sent nearby birds flapping into the air. A gust of wind stirred the trees. Josiah was surrounded by applause.

A hand on his arm grabbed Red Eagle's attention. His scouts had returned.

"Claiborne has retreated to Fort Mims," Little Warrior said. "All his men are with him."

"Good," Red Eagle's soul lifted on wings of rage. "They made war on us at Burnt Corn. Now, it is time to bring war to them."

He strode across the camp to where Josiah stood. His brother stepped aside, letting him take his place on the stump.

"Gather your weapons," Red Eagle said. "Gather your anger. We're attacking Fort Mims."

The crowd, riled up by Josiah and his prophecies, cheered with blood-thirsty joy.

∼

Tall grass tickled Red Eagle's arms as he crept toward the front gate of Fort Mims. The stockade was nearly twelve feet high, a solid line of smoothly cut tree trunks. Trails of smoke drifted from the buildings inside. The fort was alive with the sound of people at work—the clatter of pans, the thwack of wood splitting, the chatter of conversation.

Around him, the other warriors followed in silence, eluding the sentries beneath the undergrowth. Disciplined men, men who understood the Creek tribes well enough to fear them, would have spotted their movement by now. One man could go unnoticed, but no matter how quiet they were, this mass was too big to stay undetected for long. But these men were sloppy and distracted, ignoring their duties to compare their pipes.

The defenses were sloppy, too. Only the lazy or the foolish would allow the grass to grow this high, this close to the walls. With each step, Red Eagle wondered just how close they could go undetected. Ahead, he spied a pile of sand around the gate. It clearly had not been closed in some time. They might as well have invited his men inside.

Barely twenty yards from the gate, one of the sentries

spotted the intruders.

"Hey!" the soldier shouted, raising his musket. "Who's there?"

"Now!" Red Eagle rose from his crouch and charged the gate, his warriors moving in concert. Josiah let out a blood-curdling whoop to the left. To his right, Little Warrior exploded in silence.

"Indians!" the sentry yelled. He raised his musket in a panic and fired wildly, cursing himself for missing a target now only ten yards away. He scrambled to reload, dropping his gunpowder on the ground. The other sentry heaved at the gate, which stuck on the mound of sand. Frantically, he kicked sand aside in a desperate attempt to get it shut.

"Help!" the soldier yelled.

Red Eagle swung his war ax, and the first sentry fell with a wicked *thunk*. Little Warrior ended the second as Red Eagle burst through the gate into the next soldier as he tried to raise his gun, knocking him to the ground, his musket flying to the side. The rest of the Creek warriors flowed in behind.

As the warriors spread out and rushed forward, the garrison of Fort Mims, lost in various stages of undress, rushed out to form a line, hoping they didn't forget anything. Struggling to load their muskets, they spilled out of their huts and tents. There was no organization, no sense of command, just men flailing in chaos.

It was exactly as Red Eagle had hoped.

At Red Eagle's command, Josiah and Little Warrior led their men to opposite flanks. Warriors filled in the gaps to form a net that would swallow the Americans whole. Advancing downhill, their arrows picked off men on all sides until the axes and pikes hacked their way to bloody mayhem.

Civilians hid wherever they could, surrounded by the unavoidable slaughter. Some grabbed weapons and rushed to help the soldiers, but without any training, they were cut down easily.

"Kill them all!" Josiah yelled. "Take back our lands!"

"Kill them all!" others echoed.

Red Eagle knew the Americans couldn't understand their words, but their eyes knew terror. All around, their friends were cut down by blood-drenched warriors howling in nightmarish glee.

Out of the corner of his eye, Red Eagle watched the Americans facing Josiah's flank lay down their arms and raise their hands in surrender, begging for mercy. Red Eagle spun from one ruined adversary to stick his ax in the chest of another, then watched Josiah and his men cut the surrendering men apart. Red Eagle darted in their direction.

"They've surrendered!" he barked. "Don't kill them."

One of the warriors raised his club to strike the prisoners. Red Eagle lunged forward, punched him in the side and grabbed his arm, twisting until the club fell to the ground.

"You are a warrior, not a murderer."

"They would do it to us," the man said.

"And we are better men," Red Eagle replied.

All around, Red Eagle watched his men massacring anyone in sight. Unarmed soldiers cut down as they surrendered. The injured hacked to pieces where they lay in the dirt. It sickened him to see righteous battle descend into callous murder, his own people breaking every custom of war to drive out the Americans.

Two feet away from him, a warrior raised his ax high above his head, ready to bring it down upon an injured soldier.

"Stop!" Red Eagle snapped.

He was too late. The ax fell, caving in the man's skull. A spatter of pulpy flesh hit the ground. The warrior yanked his ax out of the horror and moved on without acknowledging Red Eagle.

Two more Americans stood against the wall of a timber barracks house, their hands raised above their heads in mercy. A pair of warriors in buckskin trousers advanced on them with blood-stained clubs.

"Enough." Red Eagle grabbed the nearest of the two warriors by the shoulder. "Are we to become like them? Are we—"

Arrows whistled across the yard, burying themselves in the chests of the two soldiers. One of them stood for a long moment staring at Red Eagle, blood spilling from his lips, before collapsing in a twisted heap.

At the far end of the fort, between two huts, warriors closed in on the last group of Americans, who were using a wagon as a barricade. Muskets protruded defiantly through the gaps, and one last gasp of smoke left their guns, but it was too late.

As a white flag was flung to the sky, Red Eagle raced in between his own warriors against their bloodlust. As he neared, he saw the men were defending a group of women. His warriors advanced with murder on their minds, their weapons raised. Red Eagle intercepted the pack leader, tackling him, and grabbing him by the throat. He sprung up to glare at the rest. Standing in the space between the petrified eyes of the whites and the thundering chests of his blood-stained warriors, he raised his arms.

"Enough!" he bellowed.

At last, the Creek warriors halted, stunned at their leader's fury. Josiah lifted his ax to his shoulder and narrowed his eyes at his half-brother.

"I, more than anyone, " Red Eagle said, "have reason to want the Americans dead."

Angry cheers greeted those words, men raising their weapons in anticipation of blood.

"But we do not kill the innocent. The Breathmaker does not condone evil. We do not murder. We accept their surrender."

"You would let this coward escape death?" Josiah pointed into the crowd beneath the white flag. There stood Governor Claiborne, his face pale.

Red Eagle's hand tightened around the handle of his ax as the thought of planting it in the governor's skull flashed through his mind.

Red Eagle closed his eyes, and steeled his breath.

"Or lose a part of myself?" Red Eagle gritted his teeth. "Yes. Make space for them in the barn. They are our captives. They'll come with us."

As the Americans filed out from behind their over-turned wagon, Red Eagle saw a distinctive figure. William McIntosh averted his eyes, but there was no mistaking his jet black hair. He peeked at Red Eagle, making eye contact. The two nodded to each other. To think his men would have killed his cousin in such a way. He thought of his wife and children, and was relieved to have spared his life. Almost as quickly, anger filled him that McIntosh picked the wrong side. The fool almost got himself killed. War did strange things to loyalties.

Red Eagle addressed McIntosh. "How many of the Lower Creek were here today?"

"Less than fifty when the day began," McIntosh said.

Red Eagle nodded and looked to Josiah. They had taken Creek and American lives alike.

"William Weatherford," Claiborne stopped as he passed Red Eagle. "You are full of surprises. I… thank you for honoring the surrender."

The view of his wife's rotten skull. The blue of his baby's corpse. The rumbling fire that consumed his home. Each roared back into his head. He pictured Claiborne's head impaled on a spike above the gate as the fort was burned to the ground. Instead, the governor extended his hand in peace as if forgiving a debt. Red Eagle looked at McIntosh, whose eyes were wide and fearful, and back to the governor.

He spat on the ground at Claiborne's feet.

"You are a prisoner. Go to the barn," he said, "while you still can."

CHAPTER 13

What We Fight Against

"What the hell do you mean you don't know anything about him?"

Andrew Jackson slammed his fist against the table, rattling cups and spilling coffee onto the newspaper that lay between him and the fat man called Copperfield. The man from the War Department was flustered. He and all his chins nervously looked around the posh hotel bar. The plush leather seats and lace curtains weren't used to such clamor. Fellow patrons turned to scowl at the lean-faced soldier in his smart blue jacket. A few expressions turned to excitement upon recognition of his face.

"It's a simple statement, Colonel Jackson," Copperfield's chins wobbled. He forced a fake smile for the onlookers.

"It's General Jackson," Jackson said. "I can appreciate when a man knows he's being simple, but that doesn't help me exterminate these savage bastards. How is it that William Weatherford—Red Eagle, did you call him? How can he command a whole rebel army that took a fort without a casualty, and you've got nothing on him?"

"General, this is not like fighting the British," Copperfield returned Jackson's angry glare. "The Creek don't print newspapers reporting the exploits of their officers. They don't write editorials on their competence and character. We don't have ambassadors that meet Creek generals at balls or hear gossip about them from statesmen and whores."

"Whores with taste, I guess," Jackson sneered.

Copperfield blinked, and continued. "When you faced Pakenham, we told you he was brave and tactically minded, but a little foolhardy. Against Lambert, I reported that he lacked courage until he takes a drink. But no one outside of Alabama knows anything about Weatherford. The man's never fought in a war."

Sweat found the fat man's brow. The mere look of him—the anxious eyes, the loose fat drooping from his jaw—disgusted Jackson. And here he was, proving his worthlessness. Jackson couldn't look at him without filling with hate.

"Not against my army, at least," Jackson said.

"If you have contacts among the Indians, then I would love to hear their reports. Otherwise, you will have to rely on the settlers."

The two men stared at each other.

"I believe we're done here," Copperfield said at last. "Remember this, General." He pushed back his chair and stood, tapping the headline that lay between them. "This is what we fight against."

He turned and waddled out into the street.

Picking up the paper, Jackson read the headline once more. "Fort Mims Massacre: Hundreds Slaughtered by Savages!" The article below was hogwash, Jackson thought. Rumors that filled the void left where men used to stand. Hell,

Jackson even owed them a debt of gratitude since these words would rally support for his cause. He needed all the help he could get, and it was easier to recruit Americans to put a bullet in a redskin than to put one in the British. But he'd be damned if he relied on its intelligence.

"What do you make of this, Harding?" he asked.

"Sir?" The young lieutenant, who had stood quietly at attention throughout Copperfield's visit, sounded surprised to hear his own name.

"Take a seat, soldier," Jackson pushed one out for the lad. "Tell me what you think of this rebel, Weatherford."

Harding settled onto the chair, his back still rigid, face expressionless, only the flicker of his eyes giving away his uncertainty at how to handle his superior.

"He's smart," Harding ventured. "For an Indian, I mean."

"What makes you say that?" Jackson sat back, stretching out his long legs.

"He got in before they could shut the gate," Harding said. "Like Odysseus at Troy. Get past the walls, the hard part's done."

"Good." Jackson nodded. Unlike Copperfield, Harding had some intelligence. He was glad he'd found a good one. "What else?"

"Bloodthirsty." Harding stared down at the newspaper report, with its talk of scalping and slaughter.

"Maybe," Jackson said. "Once you've spent more time on the campaign, you'll see how cruel men can be when their blood's up. Sometimes the weapons just swing themselves. That many dead tells me he didn't stop them from killing the innocents. Either he's a cruel redskin or a weak one."

"Could a weak man take Fort Mims?" Harding asked.

"Good point." Jackson nodded. "Doubt it. We have us a cruel adversary."

A bell chimed as the door of the hotel swung open. A half-dozen men walked in, caps in hand. With worn clothes and weather-beaten faces, they didn't fit in here at all. One of them was missing an ear. They glanced about with the insecurity of men who didn't know how to act, but did know they were doing it wrong.

The leader, a tall fellow in a gray coat, caught sight of Jackson. With unsure steps, he led the party across the dining room through a sea of disapproval.

"Excuse me, sir," the man clutched his cap with calloused fingers. "Are you General Jackson, sir?"

"That I am." Jackson rose and held out his hand. "And you would be…?"

"Thomas Schaffer, sir." The man looked awestruck as he shook hands with Jackson.

"What can I do for you and these fine fellows, Mister Schaffer?" Jackson asked.

"We heard you were heading out to Alabama," Schaffer said. "To fight those damn Indians, pardon my language. Is that true, sir?"

"Yes, it is."

"We read in the paper about that massacre," Schaffer said. "Well, I read it and these boys listened. We'd like to volunteer to come with you and kill the savages."

"Mighty patriotic of you gentlemen."

All six of them smiled. They straightened, seeming to forget for a moment how out of place they were.

"The lieutenant here will take your details," Jackson said.

Harding reached into his satchel and pulled out a sheet of paper. It was the second sheet, nearly full, with over fifty names on the first. Intel said thousands more volunteered in the states and territories bordering the Creek nation.

Much was at stake, and these men knew it. Unfarmed land for the taking. Vengeance for all the brutal Indian attacks in the papers. The need of securing the nation's borders before Europeans could take what was rightfully theirs.

William Weatherford had his victory at Fort Mims. Good for him. He preferred his enemy to have hope before he bled it out of him. Weatherford might have killed every man, woman, and child there—Jackson sure as hell told people he did—but one thing was certain: Weatherford would answer for this brutality.

∽

Josiah sat by a fire at the edge of the Creek camp. All alone, he threw herbs into the flames, watching the flash of color as they burned. He breathed deeply to take in their rich, sweet scent.

Closing his eyes, he drew his attention to his breath, feeling it flowing in and out of his body as everything else faded away. The smoke from the herbs blurred the sensations still coming to him, until the sounds of the camp went dark and the ground beneath him fell away.

From the depths of his mind, images stirred. The memories of the land were reaching out to him.

In his mind's eye, Josiah stood on the edge of a cliff. Lines of warriors stretched out to either side of him as far as the distance could take them. Red Eagle was there. So were Little Warrior and all the other men who had been at Fort Mims. A familiar face lay beyond them, and after a moment, Josiah placed it: a young Broken Tree. Past him were faces from Josiah's childhood, men long gone from the ranks of the Creek nation. Beyond them stood generation after generation, stretching back beyond the memories of his people.

Beneath them off the cliff, all he could see was a dense cover of dark, swirling clouds. As the clouds rose, he realized they weren't clouds at all, but vast flocks of vultures, floating on the eddies of a fierce wind.

The first of the vultures topped the cliff, far down the line from Josiah. Suddenly, it swooped and caught a man in its claws, and carried his screams away. In rapid succession, more vultures reached the top and plucked away more of his brethren.

Josiah raised the club in his hand, ready to fight. But as he did so, he realized that the vultures were diving too fast to swing his club at them.

Only bold action could save him and the rest of the Creeks.

Raising his weapon, Josiah dove off the cliff edge, gliding to the nearest vulture. A thousand voices rose in a war cry as Red Eagle and the others followed him. Josiah wound up and with a mighty swing, he cracked the vulture's skull out of the sky.

The vision faded. Josiah opened his eyes.

As in his dream, so in reality. There was Red Eagle, his face cast into bright peaks and deep shadows by the light of the flames. Another sign from the spirits.

Josiah leaned forward to share his excitement with his

half-brother.

"I had a vision. The spirits have reached out to me again."

Red Eagle nodded, his expression unreadable.

"Danger comes for us, but we must attack first," Josiah said. "If we wait for them to arrive, we will be picked off piece by piece. Our people will vanish, and the memory of our people with them."

"Attack?" Red Eagle asked.

"Yes." Josiah nodded. "What we achieved at Fort Mims. We must repeat it or else the white man will steal our lands."

"I do not wish to repeat Fort Mims." Red Eagle rose, his voice a growl as deep as any bear in woods. "That was horror."

"We took Fort Mims!"

"And we lost our humanity." Red Eagle turned away. "If that is what your visions demand, I want no part."

"You reject the will of the Breathmaker?" Josiah asked, aghast at such rejection of the Creek ways. He had always known that some part of his half-brother was weakened by his white heritage, but this was unthinkable. Not now.

"Is this the word of the Breathmaker," Red Eagle asked, "or the man with a taste for slaughter?"

"You lived too long in a comfortable home," Josiah bit back the worst of his fury at the insult. "I have seen the world for the harsh place it is. A force of evil can only be stopped by a stronger force. Any true Creek can see that."

"I know the harshness of this world, more than you ever will. I will not give others the same fate."

Red Eagle turned his back and strode away.

Josiah glared into the fire. He reached for another log, and flung it on top. A shower of sparks erupted, coiling upward in smoke.

~

The prisoners huddled in the darkness of the wooden hut. The windows were boarded up. Light crept in where it could, but it didn't bring any warmth with it. At least Red Eagle had made sure they had blankets, bandages for their wounds, and enough food and water to see them through.

"I'm going to kill them all," Governor Claiborne growled, smacking his heel against the dirt floor. "When I get out of here, I'm going to raise fresh troops and cut all their savage heads off. Shoulda killed me while he had the chance."

"There are ladies present, Governor," McIntosh said.

He glanced across at his sister-in-law, Mary, sitting next to the locked door. A stripe of light crossed her shoulders. Despite their surroundings, she looked as hearty and vital as ever with her rosy cheeks. She let out a small smile, but as the governor blustered an apology, she rolled her eyes.

"Seen a massacre before," Mary said. "Never been locked up in a barn, though. Hardly think a few curses will unsettle me."

"See, McIntosh," Claiborne said. "There's no need for your Indian-loving sensitivities when—"

There was a clunk as the bar was drawn back from the outside of the door. Claiborne skittered in cowardice across the dirt behind the nearest woman.

The door opened, blinding the hut in harsh sunlight. Three silhouettes, weapons in hand, stood in the door frame.

"William McIntosh and Mary Stiggins," one of the men said. "Red Eagle summons you."

Warily, McIntosh stood, and made his way to Mary. He helped her onto her feet and led her out the door.

CHAPTER 14

Dinner Conversation

An American newspaper sat in Red Eagle's hand, neglected. This war proved to him that the news was a lie sold as the truth. A nation at war didn't want to read the truth. It wanted to believe the story that most benefited the nation. It all sickened him, but before he could read the headline, his eyes found the fire.

Flickering in the hearth, it thundered like a team of horses racing from certain death. With every crack in a log, the image of fire burst into his head. The fires that swallowed his home, the fires that engulfed Fort Mims. It was painful and it was brutal and it was even worse when he closed his eyes. He couldn't escape the image that would be forever burned into his mind. He couldn't forget the charred piles of innocents. Not the women and not the tiny hands of the children.

Josiah had lost his way. Since calling himself The Prophet, he escalated the warriors' violence to monstrous levels. Red with blood and rage, he was becoming obsessed with the idea that full slaughter was the answer. He no longer spoke of driving back the settlers, but of cleansing the land. Nothing good comes from raging fury. It wasn't a question of whether

Josiah needed to be controlled, but how.

The image of Claiborne, the memory that he was still alive, stirred him and, for a moment, he thought perhaps Josiah was right after all. His heart roared at the memory of his family, their blood almost certainly on Claiborne's snarling hands. He had never hated anything as much as he hated mercy in that moment. If only his men hadn't slaughtered the innocents, he would have killed him and not thought twice about it. Was it murder to kill a murderer, or was it justice?

A knock on the door drew him back into the small village cabin. It was well kept and warm. The rich smell of venison stew bubbled from a pot over the fire.

"Enter," he said.

"Your guests," Little Warrior swung the door open.

William McIntosh entered, trying to hide a limp in his left leg. His trousers were torn and crusted with dried blood. A bandage bulged beneath. He was dirty and unshaven, but he had his wits intact.

A tension held both men in its grip. Here they were, kin and old friends, enemies in a battle that could easily have killed them both. It felt strange to recognize the face of the enemy in someone you love.

McIntosh was trailed by a hearty woman with red cheeks and light brown hair. She was no beauty, but she was alright, and walked with a grace that got exactly what it wanted. She offered a polite, yet sincere smile that arrested Red Eagle.

"Cousin," McIntosh looked around suspiciously.

Red Eagle couldn't look away from the woman.

"I don't believe you've met my wife's sister, Mary Stiggins."

"What? Oh, the guards told me who you were," Red Eagle

said to Mary. "William's family is my family."

"Thank you, General Weatherford." Mary curtsied.

"Not general," Red Eagle was amused.

"You command an army, do you not?" Mary asked.

"The European and Creek ways of war aren't the same," Red Eagle gestured toward a solid oak table and chairs. "Please, I hoped we might share dinner." He looked at Little Warrior. "Will you stay?"

The scout shook his head. "Patrols," was all he said before he closed the door from the outside.

"Found someone less talkative than you," McIntosh sat down. Resting in his seat with a wince, he was fighting back a lot of pain, but the hit on his pride seemed worse than on his body. He couldn't bear to face his cousin, and stared into his hands instead. Mary's eyes looked expectantly at her brother-in-law. Nothing.

"You may be a prisoner," Red Eagle fetched the pot from the fire and ladled the stew into bowls, "but I didn't invite you in here to eat silently. Cousin, tonight, you're my guests."

"Thank you," Mary took a seat across from her brother-in-law. "Without you, we would both be dead."

"Wish I had done better, more might have lived." Red Eagle set the pot down and cut slices of bread from a crusty loaf.

"You don't have to apologize," McIntosh said. "I was there. I saw what you did. We all did. The best you could. All of us in that hut know you saved our lives…" McIntosh's voice wavered as a tear found his eyes. "And you didn't have to."

"After the way we parted last," Red Eagle held his gaze as he found the seat opposite, "I was not sure…"

"I was mad at us both, mad at this idiocy we've gotten

sucked into, but that doesn't mean..." Red-faced, McIntosh shook his head, and left his thought unfinished. He picked up his spoon, dipped it in the stew, and took a bite. The flavor invigorated him. "Good. You hunt the meat yourself?"

Red Eagle nodded.

"You'd have gotten more if I'd been there," McIntosh said.

"Yes, we'd also have a wild chicken or two."

McIntosh looked up to his cousin. Mary watched, uncertain. Then, the two men laughed. It was the start to an unlikely but valuable feast. Though Mary was invited because she was close to McIntosh, Red Eagle found that he was enjoying her company for its own sake. She was as fiery and quick to offer an opinion as her brother-in-law, but was open to discussion. She was considerate. But warm thoughts only live as long as nostalgia for childhood memories. It was impossible to avoid the subject of war.

"Your government and the settlers must be made to understand that, terrible as this is, it is their fault," Red Eagle said.

"Mister Weatherford," Mary dropped her spoon into her empty bowl. "That is pure hokum."

"*Hokum*?" Red Eagle regarded her. It wasn't a subject he was willing to bend on, so why was he smirking? He hadn't heard anybody disagree with that view since the war started. Not even McIntosh, as was showing on his face. "Please enlighten the rest of us."

"Tecumseh only came to you because the British recruited him to open up another front on their war with us. You're both just pawns of the British Empire."

"I do not fight for Tecumseh," Red Eagle said. "I fight for

me."

"So I'm to believe the British played no part in why we find ourselves on opposite ends of the table?"

He leaned back, wondering what to say. She had a point. He hated that she had a point. But that did not stop her from being right. "Whatever happened elsewhere, here, in these woods, it was the Americans who brought war to the Creeks."

"You've been married, Mister Weatherford, just like I have." A teary sorrow momentarily seized Mary's eyes. "If marriage taught me one thing, it's that it takes two sides to start a fight. Any fool can be wrong, but it takes two fools to war over it."

"This is no domestic squabble," Red Eagle said.

"No, it isn't. But do you expect me to believe no one on your side was itching to go to war on 'the white man'?"

Red Eagle thought about Josiah, Tecumseh, and other belligerent members of the Red Stick faction. "There always are, but they are not in charge."

"You see?" Mary said. "If your people weren't as violent and hateful as our side, we wouldn't be at war." She leaned back and awaited his response.

"Perhaps," Red Eagle said. "But Claiborne has done unforgivable things."

"Like massacring helpless prisoners?"

"Mary." McIntosh reached out and laid a hand on her arm. "I don't think this is a topic we should—"

"It is." Mary's words had stirred the hurt and rage inside Red Eagle, but that wasn't something he could shy away from. He felt his heart race, his breath deepen, and darken. He had to face the reality of this war and of himself. He disagreed with her, but her boldness forced him to follow her logic. "The path I tread is cast in deep shadow. I will take what illumination I can."

"Good grief, now war's made you a poet?" McIntosh yawned widely and rubbed his eyes. "Sorry, haven't been sleeping well. We've got blankets, not beds, and this leg..."

"Please." Red Eagle pointed to his cot in the corner of the room.

McIntosh's eyes went wide, and his mouth started to water. "Well, I won't say no." McIntosh limped over to the bed and threw himself down. Red Eagle and Mary lowered their conversation. Snoring quickly filled the room like a blunt saw to a log, and they spoke even louder than before.

"War has not changed him," Red Eagle's heart warmed by the familiarity of McIntosh's presence, even in the form of that sound.

"It changes us all," Mary said. "He's just good at hiding it."

"Do you disagree with everything that's said to you, or just when I say it?"

"I've been accused," she started, sadness filling her eyes, her gaze falling to the floor.

"Your husband?" Red Eagle asked quietly, wary of intruding on grief, yet aware that even he had needed to talk about it.

Mary nodded.

"He was killed by Cherokee," she looked up at him with a challenge in her eyes. "A land dispute some years back."

"I'm sorry. You must miss him." He didn't have to ask. He knew. Just like how he would miss Sapoth until his dying day.

"I still love him. That never dies."

She brushed a tear from the corner of her eye, and Red Eagle found himself doing the same. McIntosh rolled over, breaking wind to snap the silence. They tried to keep their laughter quiet.

"Has he always sounded like a pig when he sleeps?" Mary asked.

"Always," Red Eagle replied. "Almost got us killed on a hunting trip once. Let's see, it was the edge of winter…"

Deep into the night, they traded stories to a score of a crackling fire and deep, guttural snores.

CHAPTER 15

A Show of Good Will

William McIntosh still couldn't see. Sounds were his only guide through the blindfold. Birds conspiring in the trees. The hypnotic stroke of a paddle in the water. The distant, then deafening, roar of rapids over rocks was followed by an eerie silence. What once sounded like home now frightened him to the bone. He knew Weatherford wouldn't kill him, but was he with them? More importantly, was he really safe in the hands of his men?

All of a sudden, their canoe jolted to a halt in a crunch of stones. Wherever they were, they had reached the bank. He would find out soon enough. Now, all he could hope for was to not fall in. On a bitterly cold morning like this, falling into the water would make the rest of the day unbearable.

"Take off your blindfold," a voice said.

McIntosh removed his blindfold and examined his surroundings. He had definitely been here before. How long had they been paddling? He looked for the sun, but it was too low to see. Almost an entire day. They were still in the Alabama Territory. He surely had made it home from here before, wherever the hell here might be.

The trees were bare, their leaves rotting to a sludgy mulch at their roots. Frost looked like a ghostly warning from the tree branches. The spirits were making a statement.

Red Eagle helped him out of the canoe. Down the shore, Little Warrior prodded Governor Claiborne to exit on his own, without granting permission to remove his blindfold first. Claiborne's first step landed in the cold water, and he tried to compensate but tripped and fell to his hands and knees. The mud was freezing. The assembled braves lent him jeers. Claiborne pushed himself to his knees and ripped off the blindfold. He first looked behind him. It was Little Warrior.

"So much for good will, Weatherford," he said.

Red Eagle stalked over and grabbed the governor by his crumpled lapels, suspending him off the ground.

"Good will," Red Eagle growled, "is the only reason you're alive."

Claiborne was petrified. Weak, he avoided Red Eagle's eyes, and began to shake. At least, he had the good sense to keep his mouth shut.

"Thank you for your mercy," McIntosh laid a hand on Red Eagle's shoulder. Were he in Red Eagle's shoes, he'd murder the bastard right there. McIntosh might even applaud it, but for now, the best case scenario was survival, even if Claiborne carried his shame with him. If Claiborne kept his mouth shut a little longer, he might live today, but they both knew Red Eagle would haunt him every day for the rest of his life. Lord knows he deserved it. "It's the right thing to do," McIntosh added.

"Do you understand your mission?" Red Eagle asked.

"You released the two of us as an offer to compromise," he said. "The Creek people and the United States have lived in peace before. You are ready to negotiate a peace treaty as long as all the settlers, all the local governors, and the politicians in the capital are firmly bound by it."

"Next fort is five miles that way," Red Eagle loosed his grip on Claiborne, and pointed north along the river. "Little Warrior will escort you there, in case of trouble."

"Thank you." McIntosh shook Red Eagle's hand.

Claiborne opened his eyes a peek, and found his footing.

"If you try to run, he will hack you to pieces." Claiborne flinched at the threat.

"What will happen to Mary?" McIntosh asked. "To the others?"

"Two is enough."

"Then we'll be on our way." Without waiting for the governor to get himself killed, McIntosh started the cold march north.

∼

McIntosh stared at the newspapers spread out in front of him. Each headline was more sensationalist than the last.

"Massacre at Fort Mims!" one read.

"Savage Terror," declared another.

"No Peace. No Mercy," demanded a third.

The articles were even worse, filled with fabricated accounts of the attack that claimed the Creek burned children alive, impaled women on spikes, and forced American soldiers into hand-to-hand combat to the death for their own amusement.

"...and yet here you are alive!" Major Whitby, the officer running the fort, set a glass down in front of McIntosh, drawing his attention back to the conversation. "Extraordinary!"

"We were lucky," Claiborne admitted, "that we were able to escape."

"William Weatherford freed us," McIntosh said. "He wants to talk peace."

"Peace?" Major Whitby asked. "With those savages? Surely not."

Half a dozen officers sat around the major's dining table facing the survivors. The contrast between the groups was stark. Cigars and whiskey served as the centerpiece as the men leaned into exquisite chairs, their buttons gleaming out of their perfectly pressed uniforms. Between plumes of smoke, they regaled in the horrors before them, oblivious to the fear they would meet on the battlefield, while a sip of whiskey was never far behind. Nearby, a roaring fire thawed McIntosh and Claiborne, who were too busy shivering to partake. Outside the window, new recruits marched asynchronously across the parade ground while a sergeant hollered abuse from the sideline.

Whitby turned his questioning gaze upon Governor Claiborne—not just a survivor of Fort Mims, but the political and military superior here.

McIntosh waited tensely to see how Claiborne would respond. He thought of Red Eagle, of how magnanimous it was to show mercy to the man who raped and murdered his wife and who executed his infant child. If a man could find the strength for peace above his own needs, perhaps Claiborne could show even a modicum of understanding.

"The request is nonsense, of course." Hate glittered in Claiborne's eyes. "The American people cannot accept a truce after this." He waved one of the newspapers.

Around the table, the officers murmured their agreement, while McIntosh sank in disappointment. Without the governor on his side, there was no hope for peace. He hated himself for believing Claiborne wanted to do the right thing. All he wanted was to win. In that moment, he realized the governor only became powerful because he was vile. Suddenly, McIntosh felt in total danger. The odd man out in a room of angry men.

"This savagery must be punished," Claiborne continued, reaching for the whiskey. "The official policy is that the red man must be disciplined. The horrors that McIntosh and I witnessed... They must suffer."

McIntosh shook his head, and looked down to conceal his rolling eyes. Sensing his cohort felt differently, Claiborne changed tack. "Think of the Lower Creek and my brave man here. McIntosh, how would you feel if we were to reward Red Eagle's violence with the same friendship we offer your people?"

The murmurs of agreement were louder this time, and Whitby banged his glass on the table in applause.

"That's the spirit," Whitby declared. "Militia men are gathering all across the neighboring states. They've heard the stories. They're thirsty for Indian blood, I tell you."

"What about the other captives?" McIntosh asked coldly. "Weatherford still has nearly twenty prisoners, including my sister-in-law. Members of my tribe. You believe he's such a savage, how can you ignore the others? We must talk peace to get them back alive."

"You're the fool who claims he is civilized," Claiborne said. "If you're right, then they don't need rescuing."

"He's not the only one there," McIntosh's chair thudded to the floor as he rose to his feet. "Are you going to risk all those lives for your own pride?"

"This is insubordination!" Claiborne said. "I should have you locked up!"

"Please, gentlemen." Whitby held up his hands. "You're both tired. You've been through a terrible ordeal. Let's not have you turn against each other now."

Claiborne stared daggers as he filled up a glass of whiskey and knocked it back. McIntosh shut his eyes and took long, deep breaths to gather his thoughts.

"Perhaps the president and other governors will treat this request more seriously," McIntosh said.

The militia officers glanced at each other, their awkward gazes finally settling on Whitby.

"I'm afraid there's no chance of that," he said. "I can sympathize with everything you've been through, but I'm afraid that your sister-in-law will have to rely on force of arms, not force of words. My higher ups simply won't consider a negotiation. Especially with a demon like Weatherford."

"Weatherford didn't do this," McIntosh insisted. "He tried to stop it."

"Hearsay," Whitby's expression showing how little he believed it. "If you want to help, the best thing you can do is to follow the Governor's lead and return to service. Gather more men in your unit, win the war, and kill that son of a bitch."

CHAPTER 16

A King's Welcome

Red Eagle looked over the letter one more time. It did not surprise him, but it was painfully disappointing.

"You didn't really believe they would make peace, did you?" Josiah asked him. The rest of the elders around the campfire kept their silence.

"I was not sure they would even respond." Red Eagle crumpled up the letter and threw it into the fire. The paper charred and ignited, transforming into a blackened shell and crumbling to ash. "But I had to try."

"No, my brother." Josiah placed a hand on Red Eagle's shoulder. "What you had to do was fight."

"You have led us to great success already, Red Eagle," Broken Tree said. "Continue as you have and all will be well."

Around the campfire, men voiced their praise for Red Eagle. His sagging spirits lifted.

Beyond them, other fires kept the Red Stick rebels warm in the darkness of winter. The clouds above, which had kept away the warmth of sunlight all day, now held in what little remained. Red Eagle looked around from fire to fire. Everywhere, men shivered in their blankets, sitting perilously close to the flames.

"Sleep now," Red Eagle said to those around him. "Tomorrow we march on Mobile." As the others rose to find their beds, he stared into the fire. When it was only the fire and him, he pulled a well-thumbed book from his pocket: the Prussian military manual his father left him. He had much studying to do.

∼

Mobile spread out below them, a mass of tightly packed streets along the side of the bay, ships drifting lazily in toward the docks. The most important city in the Southeast. Could it possibly be as easy as it looked? Peering down from a wooded hilltop, Red Eagle could only hope.

"We're back." Little Warrior's voice emerged from the bushes next to Red Eagle.

"I heard you coming that time."

"No, you did not."

"No, I did not," Red Eagle smiled. "What do you have to report?"

"It is defenseless," Little Warrior said. "The soldiers were called away to hunt us. No barricades have been prepared. The fortress is lightly manned and far from where we would begin the attack."

"Then soon it will be ours."

With Little Warrior at his side, Red Eagle headed back through the woods. Soon they were in the nearest camp, where other commanders were waiting.

„Well?" Menawa asked. One of the most senior men there, the massive warrior was as powerful a force as the Creek nation had. He had just joined up with the larger Creek forces after leading skirmishes toward the north. This was not a man who operated in the dark. He expected answers.

"Mobile lies open," Red Eagle said. "We move in tonight."

"Excellent." Menawa hefted a heavy war ax and grinned. His hooked nose gave him the appearance of a deadly bird of prey always on the hunt for his next victim.

There was a commotion at the far side of camp, warriors raising their weapons as horsemen emerged from the woods. All three were white men wrapped up in great coats, their faces concealed beneath scarves and hats. Their boots were too polished to be vigilantes. They raised their hands as muskets were leveled at them and descended from their horses on command.

"Enemy scouts," Menawa growled.

Red Eagle didn't get that sense. This was not how scouts acted.

Marching at gunpoint toward the gathered commanders, one of the men lowered a hand and unraveled the scarf covering his face, revealing a familiar black mustache.

"Señor Cardona," Red Eagle recognized the Spanish agent. He gave a wave and the sentries returned to their posts, turning the new arrivals from captives to guests.

"Red Eagle," the Spaniard gave a small bow. "How are the guns we sent you?"

"Good," Red Eagle turned to the others. "You agree?"

"Good," Josiah agreed with a nod.

"Most excellent." Menawa held up his musket. "I shot one man with this at Fort Mims, then beat another to death with the opposite end. Sturdy and accurate. Many thanks."

"Of course." Cardona made another small bow. The men behind him exchanged restrained smiles.

"And now you have brought troops?" Red Eagle asked.

"That is why I am here." Cardona flicked back the tails of his coat, then settled himself on the log beside Menawa. "I am afraid there has been a complication."

"Complication?" Red Eagle's gaze fixed on the Spanish agent. He would need to study Cardona's face. The man had been so accommodating in the past, he had almost forgotten that he was a spy, a professional liar. Suddenly, the man's every movement felt suspicious.

"Spain and the United States are not officially at war yet," Cardona said. "Until then, we cannot provide troops. When the moment comes, of course we will be with you, but not until then."

Red Eagle said nothing. He just waited for the Spaniard to say more while the other Creek leaders tensely waited. In the past, Red Eagle had found that everyone talked if you stayed silent long enough, and the secrets that broke the silence were the most valuable.

But Cardona was not most men. He sat as silent as Red Eagle, watching and waiting. The spy wasn't saying a damn thing.

"Very well," Red Eagle said at last. "We will take Mobile on our own."

"No," Cardona's gaze was steady. "That cannot happen yet either."

"No European man tells us what to do." Menawa was on his feet. "We are here, we are ready, and if Red Eagle says we take that town, then that town is ours."

"Red Eagle will not give that order." Cardona drew a slim cigar from his pocket and took his time lighting it. After a few long, luxurious puffs of smoke he spoke again. "Spain is not at war with the United States. If you seize Mobile now, then we will not have anyone to occupy it as discussed. This war will take you elsewhere, and it will fall back into American hands. Nobody wants that. You will bide your time, and when we are ready, you will seize Mobile."

Menawa grabbed Cardona by the scruff of his neck, hauling him up so that his boot tips dangled inches above the ground. Cardona's men reached for their weapons, but Little Warrior stepped toward them, shaking his head. They relaxed.

"We seize what we want," Menawa growled, shaking the dangling spy. "We kill what we want."

Cardona brought the cigar to his mouth, took a deep drag on it, and blew smoke in Menawa's face. The Creek chieftain's cheeks burned red, and he looked as if he would snap the arrogant Spaniard in half.

"You like your gun, yes?" Cardona asked. "You would like more like it? Ammunition? Food and blankets to survive? Then, do as I say."

Menawa's eyes bulged as he closed his hand around Cardona's throat. For the first time, the Spaniard looked nervous.

"Put him down," Red Eagle said.

Menawa looked from him to Josiah, who sat watching. Finally, he dropped Cardona to the ground.

With slow, purposeful steps, Red Eagle approached the Spanish agent. Overhead, birds were circling beneath a gray sky. A storm was coming in.

"This is a betrayal," Red Eagle said.

"It is an accident of timing." Cardona blew out a stream of smoke. "Stay the course."

"You encouraged us to begin this war," Red Eagle drew within inches of Cardona's face. "You told us that we were allies. That you would fight with us. That we could rely on you. Does a white man never tell the truth?"

"I can sympathize with your position," Cardona shrugged. "But we have done our best."

Red Eagle reached out and took the cigar from between Cardona's fingers. He held it up to Cardona's jacket, and lightly pressed it to the cloth, making the Spaniard squirm as it burned through the fabric.

"Without you, we are outnumbered, outgunned, out-supplied," he said. "Without you, we are surrounded by enemies. That is not the work of the King of Spain. It is your work, Señor Cardona."

Cardona winced from the cigar's heat and withdrew, tripping back over the log, and falling to the cold mud. Stained and shaking, he scrambled to his feet. He looked at his coat, where a hole exposed his burned skin. He looked to his men, and all three scurried to their horses.

"This is why I like you!" Menawa slapped Red Eagle on the shoulder. "Strong in spirit, not just body."

Red Eagle shrugged. "He is a royal con man."

Rising from his seat, Josiah looked around the assembled commanders. "American, Spanish, English, they are all the same. Mosquitoes sucking the blood from our land. The spirits are on our side. They are the only allies we need."

The others nodded their approval. Smiles returned to

their faces. But not to Red Eagle's. He knew better.

Without foreign aid, the fight was already lost.

"Forget Mobile," he said. "While the Spanish find their courage, we will find another target."

CHAPTER 17

Help is on the Way

This was not what Jackson expected.

Before him, tents were sprawled out in a slovenly, irregular mess. The entire place smelled of rotten excrement. Clearly no one thought the better of digging proper latrines or compost. Were this summer, the camp would be filled with more flies than men. The militia camp was a ragged shamble; a shamble that reeked of human waste.

As for the motley group of men who lived like this, they made Jackson's small column of volunteers look like the finest soldiers ever fielded. No one was training, nor were they attempting to bring order to the camp. All around, men slouched near their fires or in their tents. When a man finally marched up and saluted him, Jackson was surprised.

"Compliments of Governor Claiborne, sir," the man said. "He invites you to join him at the officers' club."

"Officers' club? This should be good," Jackson dismounted to follow the messenger through the camp. Harding, trailing behind, looked as disgusted as Jackson.

Reaching a log cabin on the edge of the woods, Jackson and Harding were led inside. The door slammed shut behind them, enclosing them in a bubble of warmth and comfort. Coffee, cigar smoke, and laughter filled the room.

Only two men stood to attention as they came in. One was stout, non-uniformed, his hair jet black and thinning. The other, a slender-faced colonel with floppy curls and arched eyebrows.

"General Jackson." Another man in the gold braid of a militia commander strode over and extended his hand with a glint of arrogance.

"Governor Claiborne, at your service. A pleasure to have you here to help us," Claiborne said.

"Not to help, Governor." Jackson gestured and Harding handed over their written orders. Opening the document, Jackson held it out for Claiborne to see. "To command."

Around the room, the laughter died as men caught Jackson's stern tone. A few more shuffled to their feet.

"I see." Claiborne's smile stiffened. "Of course. Anything I can do to help you, General, you need only ask. I like to think that I know the local situation."

"What you can do, sir, is stay out of my way." There was utter silence as Jackson glared at Claiborne. "This camp is a disgrace. You are a disgrace. The mess you have made, politically and militarily, is a disgrace that stains the halls of government. I would have you locked in irons and lashed at the post, but then you'd actually be serving a purpose."

"How dare you!" Claiborne pointed his finger in Jackson's face. "Without me there would be no militia here, no campaign to fight!"

"You're right. Without you, there would be no fight here, no men would have to give their lives fighting for a drunken buffoon," Jackson said. "Now get out of my command post."

Claiborne looked around the room, his face falling as he realized that no one would catch his eye. His comrades could see where power laid, and no one wanted a part of the loser.

Shoulders slumping, he trudged out of the cabin, letting the door slam shut behind him.

Jackson turned to the men who had first stood to attention.

"Colonel, get out there and find a bugler. Have the men assembled to begin drills in ten minutes."

The colonel glanced at the non-uniformed man next to him. "Tell him, McIntosh," the colonel said. "It's not our doing."

"Sir," McIntosh said, "there are no buglers. General Claiborne considered them a low priority."

"I see." Jackson closed his eyes, fighting back a curse against Claiborne's idiocy. "And you, McIntosh, are you the Creek Chief who stayed loyal?"

"I am, sir."

"How well do you know our enemy?" Jackson said.

"Some better than others."

"I heard you are well-versed in both sides' method of war?"

"I am," McIntosh said.

Jackson looked McIntosh up and down, then nodded. "Gather whichever men pass for sergeants around here and have them use their voices. We'll find some buglers later."

"Sir." McIntosh left.

"What's your name, Colonel?" Jackson asked the other man.

"Coffee, sir," the colonel replied. "John Coffee."

"And I thought coffee would come in a tin cup." Dutiful laughter followed Jackson's comment, even as he caught Coffee's expression, a forced smile on the man's lean features, and realized how many times he must have heard that joke. "Tell me about the state of our forces, Colonel Coffee. And please speak freely—I value honesty."

"Freely speaking, sir," Coffee said, "the state of our forces is even worse than it looks."

Jackson winced. How could it possibly be worse?

Coffee continued, "There's been no drill and no discipline. We have volunteers on short contracts from all over the surrounding areas. They have no experience of fighting together, or at all. They are ill-equipped, under-fed, and mutinous. They need licking into shape, but I fear they will snap if we try it."

"Not if, Colonel Coffee," Jackson said. "And not try. When we do it."

Men were shouting orders outside the cabin.

"Gentlemen." Jackson turned to the rest of the officers. "Let's make an army."

∽

The breath of half a dozen men and their horses frosted the dawn air. Jackson didn't mind being in the saddle this early, he just wished this wasn't the thing that had forced him to it.

"Are you sure you don't want troops to back us up?" Coffee asked. He sat on his horse with the confidence of a man born to it, just like McIntosh and the other two officers. Harding was determined as always to impress, but his horse knew better.

"We can't win this one with numbers," Jackson said as the tramp of boots approached around the corner of the woodland road. "It's authority or nothing."

The volunteers slowed their pace as they rounded the corner and saw the officers waiting for them. Still they trudged on, some with boots falling apart on the frozen dirt, until they stood directly in front of the thin line of horses. Jackson counted fifty or so. Most of them awfully lean.

"I hear that you men are deserting," Jackson's voice carried across the crowd.

"We're leaving," the leader replied. "You've got to be a soldier to desert, but soldiers get fed and soldiers get paid. We've haven't seen money or a proper meal in a month."

"Gentlemen, your complaints are fair," Jackson said. "You are free men. Free to do as you see fit. I, on the other hand, am a soldier. I do as I am told, and sometimes that means being rather brutal. Some say it's what I'm best at. But brutality doesn't solve hunger. It doesn't put clothes on your back. I am disappointed to learn that you've been mistreated. That they didn't train you to kill Indians. Or pay you the money for killing Indians. I won't make you stay.

"I promise you that food is on its way. Along with boots and muskets, too. I've spent my own money making sure that any of my men have what they need.

"I dare say you've heard enough promises to last a lifetime. You've no more reason to trust me than you had to trust that coward Claiborne, and he never forced you out of your tents at dawn to march back and forth."

The soldiers looked at him uncertainly. These weren't the sort of words that they had expected, yet still they lingered, expectant. Jackson knew this moment well.

This was the moment where he either won or lost.

"All I will ask is this," Jackson said. "Did you come here to make an easy wage to take back home? Or did you come here to protect our communities from the men who committed murder at Fort Mims? Maybe you came here for the chance to kill Indians.

"I know that's why I'm here. If you are too, then I ask you for one more month. Food is on the way. Boots are coming. Weapons are coming. And thanks to McIntosh and Colonel Coffee, the training you need to use those weapons is right here.

"The choice is yours, men. I hope you feel the same. And if not... well, there's the road. It's twenty-seven miles to the next town."

He backed his horse up to the side of the track and the other officers did the same. The would-be deserters looked uncertainly at him, then at the road, and then at the man leading them.

"All right," the leader said at last. "We'll give you two more weeks."

CHAPTER 18

Comfort Through Loss

The Red Stick rebel camp grew in number every day. They flocked to fight the American scourge, even after the rest of the world turned its back on them. It baffled Red Eagle. Their war was already lost, yet he was the only one who could tell.

The British messenger didn't even bother dismounting from his horse. Behind his drooping blond mustache, his expression carried an apologetic sadness as he looked around at the scene. The fabric of the mismatched tents barely clung on. Temporary cabins built with frozen mud didn't fare much better. The sight did not portend a promising war.

"I'm sorry, old chap, but it just can't be done anymore," he said. "We thought that we would have handed the Americans a sound beating by now, but Napoleon has us busy in the Peninsula again. We simply cannot afford our efforts in the Americas while the French threaten us at home."

"You promised us support," Red Eagle said.

"And we've given what we can. The soldiers we have are in the north with Tecumseh. The Royal Navy is occupied chasing American blockade runners. If we could do any more for you, I assure you, we would."

"You are a better liar than the Spaniard."

"I wish that I could stay and convince you." The Englishman turned his horse's head. "But I'm afraid there's a barge waiting at the river and we must reach the coast before dusk tomorrow. I wish you the best of luck and I hope that our next meeting is in better circumstances. The King sends his best."

As the Englishman disappeared through the trees, rain started to fall. The ground would be even more sodden tomorrow, and the quagmire looked intent on swallowing them whole. All the braves and all their families would have to move in this horrible cold.

As he returned to his hut, Red Eagle saw Mary Stiggins watching him from under a tree, a shawl drawn up to keep her head dry. After a moment's hesitation, he approached her.

"You heard?" he asked, pointing toward where the English spy had disappeared.

"No," Mary said. "But I can guess. The English have deserted you, too."

Red Eagle debated how to respond. Sooner or later, Mary would be sent back to the Americans, and with her, the secret of the Spaniards and the British. Perhaps he shouldn't let the information out, and hope the British were shamed into fulfilling their promise of help. Politics were not his game, so he looked at Mary, and felt something in his chest as rain spilled off his chin.

"Miserable out here, isn't it? Why don't we go inside?"

Red Eagle nodded, and led the way back to his hut. No one else took a step, but suspicious stares followed Mary the entire way. It wasn't much warmer inside. They labored to remove their boots just inside the door, only to find their feet were coated in mud. Mary trembled.

"Sit," Red Eagle removed his Prussian war manual and a half-finished moccasin from the table.

He headed to the fireplace and immediately got to work. He uncovered the ashes, discovering embers underneath. He piled on kindling and fire soon took hold. Steadily he added more fuel, building the fire before adding a pot of water.

"I imagine that you were a good husband," Mary watched him from a seat by the fire.

It was not a role he had played for some time now, but it was one he had practiced. The memory of Sapoth's corpse and their burning home flashed in his head.

"There have been better," Red Eagle said.

He sat in another chair beside her, the two of them stretching their feet out to dry in the warm from the flames.

"I am the reason she died," he stared at the coffee pot and remembering his wife in their kitchen. "I defied Claiborne and my family paid the price."

"No," Mary said. "You did what was right. You cannot blame yourself for the terrible things another man did in response."

She placed a hand on Red Eagle's arm.

"After I lost Richard, I found one hundred ways to blame myself," she said. "What if I had not sent him into town that day? What if I had gone myself? What if I had chosen a safer place for us to settle? I found a thousand reasons why it was my fault.

"But in the end, I had to realize that others were at fault for Richard's death—the man who swung that club, the man who led those warriors in their attack, the men who taught them to do so in the first place. I had to let go of the guilt before it destroyed me."

Red Eagle stared at her, his eyes watering. "Thank you." Even in the face of sadness, he couldn't help but smile when he looked at her. Just being around Mary was comforting—an island of happiness in a sea of misery and frustration. She was a prisoner, but he did his best to make her life comfortable. He had ordered that the prisoners be allowed to leave their hut during the day—after all, if they tried to escape, they'd be worse off in the wilderness. The principle remained. They were people, they deserved to have warm clothes and warm food.

Wrapping a cloth around his hand, he picked up the steaming pot and poured them each a cup.

"I am as much a white man as I am Creek," Red Eagle was surprised to find that he could say it out loud. "I have friends on each side. I watched some of my men steal the livelihood of my neighbors. Any other time, they would be my enemies. Half my world has been ripped away from me. I chose to fight, but at times I doubt that it is right."

"Of course, you do. Only a monster could go through this without doubt. No one can see the light in the eyes of another man and honestly believe they have the right to take it away. And for you, half of one side and half the other... I cannot imagine how awful that must feel."

"Creek are fighting on both sides. The same goes for half-breeds. Half the frontier has mixed blood. Surely you aren't the only one who feels like you do."

"Perhaps," Red Eagle said. "I cannot say these things to

the men I command, so I do not know what they actually think, but I fear that, in dark times, most men harden their hearts rather than reason through doubt for a better fate. They know they must fight, so they pick a side and silence the rest."

Taking a large wooden bucket down from its hook, he poured in the water that had been boiling over the fire, then added enough cold water to make it bearable to touch. He sat it between their chairs, and sank his feet into the water. He gestured for Mary to follow, and when she dropped her feet into the water, her frozen toes brushed against his. He allowed himself a moment to appreciate the cold of a woman's feet. Even in the boil of summer, Sapoth's feet had always been frigid. Mary let out a contented sigh as the water lifted the dirt and cold from her feet.

"Thank you for this," she closed her eyes and leaning back in her chair. "It has been a dark and miserable winter. It's comforting to feel human warmth."

"Yes," Red Eagle kept his eyes on her, enjoying her smile and the gentle lines of her face. "Thank you, too, for this."

"Anytime I can bring you comfort," she opened her eyes just enough to look across at him, "you have only to ask." The warmth of the water seemed to spread up through his legs, through his loins, and into his heart.

When was the last time I felt comfort, he wondered. Didn't matter. It was wonderful no less. On this, he did not feel conflicted.

CHAPTER 19

Strength of Spirit

Had he had been living in this hut permanently, Red Eagle would have repaired it long ago. Damp seeped in, threatening the few books he had taken in raids. Wind whistled in through cracks during the night. Today, the roof groaned as it settled after another shift in the weather. After the last torrential rain, they were blessed with four bright days. Now, the rain had returned with a vengeance.

At least those dry days had given them time to act. Raids went out to harass American forces, and supplies returned. Two settler outposts were burned down, and still no casualties. He knew it wouldn't last forever. Forces from the Americans had been sent out to other camps within striking distance.

Slowly, a strategy was beginning to coalesce. The piecemeal, grinding campaign relied on their superior knowledge of the land to counter the Americans' numbers. Rumors had reached him that the Americans called upon a general called Jackson to replace the bastard Claiborne. Unlike the Governor, this man was rumored to have military successes to his name, but word was that his hatred of Indians burned even deeper. If Red Eagle was to save his comrades from disaster, he needed a way to counter that strength and experience.

"As always, we offer our thanks to Red Eagle," Broken Tree said to the war council gathered around the table. "He has led us from weakness to strength in the face of the invaders."

Menawa pounded the table in applause and soon the whole room followed suit. When he spoke, he filled the room. "You should have seen him at Little Road. I swear, he shot three soldiers from the saddle before they even saw we were there."

More cheers followed, everyone chiming in with something they had seen him do, all eager to prove that they had been there. It was a good feeling. Red Eagle couldn't help but smirk. He knew they wouldn't be happy with his next words.

As Red Eagle declared his intention to continue their slow pace of attack, he saw only three of the dozen men around the table who nodded in agreement. Others listened in reserved silence, as was the tradition of Creek elders. And then there were the detractors, the vocal ones.

"We should strike now and strike hard," Josiah pounded his fist against his palm. "The longer we wait, the more time this Jackson has to organize his forces."

"And how should we strike?" Broken Tree asked, undecided. Though he was too old to be a war leader, his voice commanded much respect. He sat wrapped in layers of blankets, recovering from the chill that had seeped into his bones on the way to the meeting.

"Raze more of their settlements," Josiah said. "Drive them away as the Breathmaker has shown in my visions. Purge this land and make it clean for the free people."

"And when the American soldiers come?" Red Eagle asked, remaining calm and still despite his frustration.

"Then we know that we have hurt them." Josiah wore a bloodthirsty grin as he looked around the circle of men sitting on rugs and stools around the small hut. "Then they chase us to a place where we choose to fight. The power of the spirits will make us stronger."

He rolled up the sleeve of his wool tunic, revealing symbols painted onto his skin in colored dye.

"I wear the magic of the spirits every time I go to battle," he said. "I have fought at every chance we have had, and I still stand. The power of the spirits is beyond doubt. They are with us."

Menawa stood, silencing the space. "You know that I believe in you, Red Eagle. I hold my men back from slaughtering the filth upon our lands because you ask. I follow your cautious strategy, weak as it makes me feel. But surely now is the time to strike, now that the spirits are on our side?"

"This is not about spirits," Red Eagle said. "It is about guns and men."

"Men… or a woman?" Josiah turned to him with an accusatory glare.

Red Eagle was taken aback, but all around the room, men were nodding their approval for what Josiah had said, even those he considered to be on his side in this.

"What do you mean?" he asked.

"That woman, Mary Stiggins," Menawa said. "You spend more time with her than with your war chiefs."

This time the agreement was vocal, a chorus of murmurs

from around the circle.

"She is our prisoner," Broken Tree said, "and we are at war. You should not become as close to her as you have."

"What does that have to do with war?" Red Eagle's hand tightening on the arm of his seat.

"War is politics," Broken Tree said. "Loyalty matters. You lead us in war, and we need your loyalty to be clear."

"Who here doubts my loyalty?" Red Eagle rose angrily to his feet, the chair clattering to the ground behind him. Had he not done what his people asked him to? What Tecumseh asked him to? "Answer me and then prove your own character with your fists."

"Perhaps it is time that you proved your character, brother," Josiah was on his feet too, arms spread wide, a pleased look on his face. "If your loyalty really is to the Creek rather than the white man, then choose a Creek woman over this prisoner. A marriage to another tribe's princess could rally more to our cause."

"No," Red Eagle snapped. "I will not marry for politics."

"So love moves you?" Josiah raised an eyebrow. "Is it the love of white faces, like the one who took our mother from the tribe?"

"Love for Sapoth," Red Eagle said. "And grief. It is too soon. Shame upon you, brother, or have you never known love?"

The groaning of the roof timbers could be heard once more as the two men stood staring at each other. No one moved. No one spoke. Who there had the right to doubt the depths of Red Eagle's grief, especially now that the war had brought losses for them all? Even so, he didn't deny Josiah's words. A marriage would certainly strengthen their cause. It might even raise their spirits in the darkness of winter. He denied it for himself more than for Sapoth, and the mention of her name here and now felt like betrayal as much as truth.

The sound of hooves announced a scouting party arriving back in camp. When no one came to the door, they knew nothing new had been learned. The Americans were still on the march, heading slowly but certainly for the heart of the Creek. Soon, the woods would be alive with the sound of boots.

"Perhaps the Prophet Josiah is right," Broken Tree said. "Strength of spirit is as important in war as strength of arms. Striking against the Americans would make our men feel brave and strong."

"Brave and strong or dead and cold?" Red Eagle asked. "What if the American troops catch us out in the open?"

"Whose side are you on?" Josiah said. Other voices rose to support his challenge.

"What if we struck directly at the American camp, then?" Menawa offered Red Eagle a pleading look.

Red Eagle's leadership hung by a thread. There were too many against him to offer nothing, and if he gave Josiah too much, his authority would snap. He worried for the prophet's frame of mind, and if the war was Josiah's to lead, there would be no holding back his bloodlust.

"Let us attack those who deserve it," Red Eagle said. "If we muster in force, we can catch Jackson on the march near Talladega. If we bloody him before he comes any deeper into our lands, perhaps he can be turned back. As Broken Tree says, strength of spirit matters—for us and for Jackson."

"Well said," Menawa slapped Red Eagle on the shoulder.

Everybody else looked to Josiah. He had rolled his eyes back in his head and his mouth dangled open as he invited in the spirits. Red Eagle wondered if he meant it, or if he was merely milking the moment to display his importance.

Even as the thought crossed his mind, Red Eagle tried to push it away. His opinion of his half-brother had sickened under the pressure of war. Even if Josiah was wrong, and he believed that to be true in his heart of hearts, he could at least be civil in both his thoughts and actions.

When the prophet's eyes opened again, Josiah nodded at those gathered.

"The spirits say that it is good," Josiah said. "It is time for a real fight."

A covenant made, the meeting dispersed. The Creek leaders were exhausted, half their energy spent in battle, the rest waging battle on one another. They needed time to rest.

"Josiah, wait," Red Eagle said as his half-brother headed toward the door.

"As you ask," Josiah turned to face him. As the last of the others left, the prophet closed the door behind them. "You wish to talk further?"

"I want us to talk properly. Like brothers."

"Here I am," Josiah spread his arms. "What would you talk about, brother to brother?"

Red Eagle took a deep breath. So much was at stake here. Faith, love, friendship, family, the future of their people. Delicate, tangled things, a cobweb frosted with spring dew. But ultimately, it came down to one request.

"I need you to stop pushing," his gaze fixed on Josiah.

"To stop pushing?" Josiah asked.

"This talk of visions and dreams, of spirits and slaughter. It is pushing people beyond the point of reason. Our methods may differ, but we fight the same fight. Surely, you can see that both are better served if our comrades can think clearly. Let us stand together. Not divided."

"What I see is a man who would give ground to our enemies rather than face what is needed to make this land ours. The spirits have shown me-"

"Enough with the spirits!" Red Eagle snapped, unable to stop himself. "You can't keep using their name to get what you want."

"It is what they want, not me."

"Really? Because I only hear one voice coming from you, and it doesn't sound holy."

Josiah's face clouded with fury.

"My visions are real," he spat. "My faith is real. You may have let your soul become stained with white ways, but mine is clean. They speak to me."

"And how convenient that they say what you want them to."

"Enough!" Josiah yelled. "You say you want to talk, and all you do is belittle me, brother, like you've done all my life. No man would stand for this."

He stormed out of the hut, slamming the door shut behind him, leaving Red Eagle equal parts ashamed and frustrated.

He had a bad feeling about this.

CHAPTER 20

The Cost of Talladega

The flats outside Talladega, browned and barren in the harsh of winter, could not look more dead. A low fog held over the horizon, and Jackson had to work to make out the colors of his militia troops and Lower Creek warriors like a patchwork quilt on its final use. *He's out there*, Jackson thought. *Red Eagle is using the damn fog to surprise us.* They appeared in the night, blocking his march. A challenge was set for dawn.

Just then, the morning sunlight peeked out of the clouds, bringing a gleam to the tips of his men's muskets. Perhaps matters were bright for America, after all. In the light, Jackson swore they almost looked like a proper army, and he drifted to the thought of what it would look like with proper finances. He equipped desperate men with organization, added a few skills, and gave them muskets. If he could direct their panic forward, he was sure their tenacity would win the day. His scouts guessed 3,000 Indians. Biggest savage force he'd ever seen. *That's a lot of Indian blood*, Jackson thought. It would all be spilled. He was ready.

Life and death. The ultimate test.

In the light, the fog hung like a blinding lantern in the

shadows. As it burned off, a forest of rebels emerged from the fog, standing still, staring at Jackson's men. The dogs bared their teeth. There must be a reason they chose this place. The flats were strategically unremarkable. Were they sending bait? He had not yet encountered Red Eagle, but he ached for the chance. Perhaps his daddy taught him some proper war games. Perhaps he deserved respect after all.

Or perhaps today he would die.

A whoop and a call launched a tirade of battle cries from the savages. *This won't spook a soldier… if only I had soldiers*, Jackson thought. He needed to strike fast. Turf flew from the hooves of Harding's horse as he galloped along the line. He was turning into quite a rider. Funny how war changes a man.

"Sir," Harding saluted. "Colonel Coffee reports that he is ready to advance on your order."

"Make the call." Jackson looked around. "McIntosh, if you would."

The Creek Chief raised a horn to his lips and blew. Like skipping a rock across a still lake, the call echoed down the line. One by one, militia units peeled off the line, and launched an attack from the civilized world.

The rebels answered the call, with the slowed advance of a hunter just before the strike. A Creek stopped in his tracks and fired his musket. A few more guns cracked, this time falling a militiaman. Shots at this distance were a fool's errand. This battle wouldn't tilt until the volley of mass fire ripped the lines apart. Was it fear, or was it madness?

Finally, the rebels sped their advance. The flirtation was over, battle had begun. Indians on the flanks stopped to fire, but everyone in the middle pulled out weapons for combat.

Battle clubs, axes. They ran out of bullets in a gun fight, Jackson thought. A quick punch of arrows felled men from at least 3 units. Indian eyes went wide and crazed as they raised their weapons and all sprinted at Jackson's men. The mist swirled around their feet, as if a wind was powering their charge.

At Jackson's signal, the American line stopped. The training had worked. Rows of men leveled their guns, clicked back their hammers, and a line of iron ripped through the air like thunder.

That first volley always shook Jackson, no matter how many battles he fought. He felt this one in the stomach. He could see it shook the advancing Creeks too. Half of them crumbled in a bloody mess, and the other half paused as if they too expected to die.

Without hesitation, his men lowered their guns to reload, then resumed the pace forward.

"Come on," Jackson muttered, watching to see where the lines would meet. "I know you've got it in you."

"Cheering on our men?" Harding asked, unable to tear his eyes away from the action.

"Oh no, lieutenant," Jackson said with a wily grin. "I'm cheering on the animals."

∼

The blood pounded in Red Eagle's veins as the two lines hit. He swung his war ax, the tip glinting as it arced through the air. The American in front of him raised his musket, catching the ax against the stock. Red Eagle kicked him in the gut, sending the man staggering back, and then turned to the next.

Here in the heart of the fighting, at the very center of the lines, Red Eagle found it easy to lose himself in the passion of war. No politics. No grief. Just blades and clubs and brutality. Hurt and hatred. Body and mind acting as one.

For as long as he could, he moved in violent mindlessness. He had no idea how many men he killed or injured. The hunter's instinct had taken over and the predator who eats is the one who doesn't quit.

With a crackling snap, Red Eagle made a skull quit, its body slumping clumsily. He was surrounded by a ring of bodies. He had played the warrior well, but he needed to play war chief. As the line of fighting moved forward, he fell behind to study the enemy lines. Whose strategy was the American going to steal this time?

The American center was driven back, the Red Sticks pushing across the fields in a wave of fury. *Was that too easy?* he wondered. He didn't have to kill nearly enough people for their line to falter. Maybe Josiah was right, and these Americans are weak amateurs. Or maybe...

He looked around. The fighting was most intense ahead of him, where the center of the two lines met. His warriors were driving the militia back, but there was still some fighting to the right and left. There the battle waged on. Something was wrong.

It was a trap. A strategy from Hannibal. A memory flashed through his head like lightning. His father used to read war stories to him by the fireside to keep him entertained in the winter. Jackson was expecting a savage, uneducated in the ways of war. Challenge accepted.

"Menawa!" Red Eagle called out. "Josiah! Little Warrior! To me!"

Swift as blood running from a wound, word reached his leaders. As they rushed to his side, the Americans pounced on the flanks, beginning to envelop the Creek warriors. A classic pincer movement. They were waiting for this.

"We are about to be surrounded," he shouted over the noise of screams, shots, and battle cries. "Josiah, take your men and push right. Menawa, you are with me on the left. We have to split and push them back."

"But the center," Menawa's brow crumpled. "We are winning."

"No. We are falling for their trap. Little Warrior, keep sharp shooters in the center. Hold back fire as long as you can. If we don't break through, we will all die. Now is the time."

∼

"Damn his eyes!" Jackson watched in consternation as his pincer movement slowed, halted, and then turned into retreat, the nervous flanks of his force driven back by the sudden onslaught of the Creeks. "So the redskin isn't a fool."

On both sides, he spotted men jumping back as they saw the line collapse. Soon they would run and then it was all over.

"McIntosh," he yelled. "Advance in the center. Split the savages in two!"

"Yes, sir!" McIntosh shouted.

The portly chief snatched the bonnet from his head and waved it in the air as he rushed to the front line of the Lower

Creek allies yelling for carnage. A bugle sounded and men stepped forward, and, for a moment, it looked like it might work.

A bullet ended the bugle cry in a sudden, sickening gurgle. From horseback, Jackson could make out McIntosh raising his own horn to his lips. But before he could bring out a tune, his body jerked, and he fell out of sight shoulder first.

"Forward!" Jackson yelled. "Keep moving forward!"

It was too late. The right flank was in disarray and many men abandoned their muskets as they turned and ran with angry savages hot on their tail. All pretense of an advance in the center had fallen with McIntosh. The line of loyal Creek was crumbling. Harding darted back and forth behind the line to the left, dressing ranks, snapping orders, and outclassing men far above his rank.

It wouldn't be enough.

"Sound the retreat," Jackson called out, turning his horse's head away from the carnage, disgusted in himself.

He had underestimated his opponent. He would never do that again. *This Weatherford is half white after all. A worthy cursed adversary.*

∽

"There," Little Warrior pointed to one non-uniformed man among the many Americans littered on the ground.

Red Eagle rushed over. The battle was on its last legs, and he watched as his men drove off the retreating Americans, but he didn't care. There, on the ground, scarlet blood trickled from the pale lips on a massive body. It was William McIntosh.

Crouching beside his cousin and friend, Red Eagle lifted McIntosh's head into his lap.

"Lost blood," Blood oozed from the ragged wound in McIntosh's chest. He winced. His jacket was soaked.

Red Eagle brushed the hair back from his friend's face. "This is not how it should be."

"How it is," McIntosh replied. He looked up at Red Eagle, lips parting in a faint smile. "If I had the chance, fight for you with all my heart."

McIntosh's eyes lost focus and he closed his eyes. His body began to fall away, his thundering chest slowing to a quiet.

Even in victory, Red Eagle's heart suffered. Amid the sea of pain, he lifted the body of his best friend and rushed to find a medicine man much too late.

CHAPTER 21

Behind Enemy Lives

Red Eagle trudged down a half-frozen mud path beneath the skeletons of trees stripped bare of their leaves. All around, his army rode in exalted triumph over the Americans. But he could not celebrate, not with the burden before him.

He didn't want to look at the body lying across his horse, but he couldn't look away. McIntosh had not woken since he'd picked him up from the battlefield. Better to keep moving forward until he reached the camp.

McIntosh's gargantuan body bounced with the horse's footsteps. His eyes remained fastened shut. The face of one of his oldest friends, of his closest family, was dangling on the verge of death all because of a war that Red Eagle led.

In their advance on Jackson, they had uprooted their main camp. It was a risky maneuver, putting them close to the Americans to facilitate their attack. Riders along the trail directed them to the new position, and it astonished Red Eagle how close they camped to the Americans. Josiah had convinced them they were unbeatable. Only fanatics would be this reckless.

He heard a warrior whoop ahead, followed by a holler.

The cacophony could only mean they had made it to camp, announcing the victory for all to hear. The entire camp rejoiced in an uproar, sending birds flapping into the air. But many men wore steel faces. War was not kind to winners or losers. Red Eagle plodded through the celebration looking for a medicine man. Unguarded, Mary was already outside the prisoner's tent, scanning the crowd.

"William?" Mary approached. "William, are you all right? Have you been wounded?"

Her face fell as she saw whose body lay across the horse.

"No," she murmured. "No, not him."

Hurrying to the horse's side, she placed her hand against McIntosh's cheek. Tears ran down her face as she stared at the pale face. Red Eagle recoiled, thinking about how he brought back the feeling of losing her husband in war. Dealing with one loss was bad enough, another would be suffocating.

"There is life still in him," Red Eagle said. "We must find him proper care."

Together they led the horse through camp. Teepees stretched up all around like a forest of strange plants. People celebrated as they walked past, at first, but became confused as they saw the body of a former prisoner lying across their leader's saddle.

Red Eagle stopped beside the nearest medicine man. "Please help, my friend."

The medicine man rose, looking up and down McIntosh's unconscious body. "No," he responded.

"What?" Red Eagle asked, his voice rising. "If you don't help him, he will die."

The medicine man sat back down without answering.

Red Eagle needed this. He needed to keep his friend alive. He had lost enough family. This war wouldn't separate them forever, not on his watch. He needed his support. It may have been selfish, but it was true.

Broken Tree limped over to the place where they sat with McIntosh, who was wrapped in a blanket. His gray hair hung loose around his shoulders, his walking stick losing a battle with arthritis.

"The elders are not pleased," Broken Tree said.

"It is the right thing to do."

"Is it worth the trouble?"

"He is our Creek brother. He is family."

Reaching into his pocket, Broken Tree pulled out a couple of twists of tobacco.

"Here," he said. "He was not a bad man. These should go with him."

Red Eagle, "He is not dead!"

Broken Tree met his eyes and nodded as he said, "Perhaps it would be better if he was."

"Red Eagle!" Josiah strode over, a gang of his followers at his back.

"The dead must be taken away and buried." Broken Tree placed the tobacco on McIntosh's chest and backed off.

Josiah stomped up to Red Eagle and stood, arms folded, glaring at him.

"Do you intend to commit sacrilege?" he asked. "Our own brothers need graves of their own, and you honor the enemy? They stole our homes and raped our land."

"He lived among us," Red Eagle said. "He is Creek. He is worthy and you know it."

"He is a traitor," Josiah said. "Part of the rot that destroys our lands, our homes, our lives. He has no place here, among warriors."

"Did the spirits tell you that?" Red Eagle asked, his voice cold and hard.

"They did not need to, but they will turn against you if you continue this sympathy for the enemy."

"I'm not one of your fanatics," Red Eagle said. "Do not tell me what to do."

"No, you're a soft half-breed who would fight for both sides. Tecumseh was wrong."

"I am here for my family."

Josiah looked at his half-brother, cradling the enemy in his lap. The prisoner Mary was kneeling over him in tears. It was a ridiculous scene. Loyalty matters in war.

"You would do well to remember where you are." Josiah gestured to the growing crowd. These were the looks of enemies. He was surrounded by fanatics.

"William." Mary touched his arm. "There is another way."

∽

Rain pummeled the blue jackets of the three militia men in the clearing. They all sat in the saddle, ready to gallop away if the meeting went south. Behind them stood a mule, its ears twitching in the rain. Through the haze of the downpour, a horse pulled toward them.

"Are you Mr. Weatherford?" the youngest man pulled a musket to his shoulder. His jacket had brighter buttons than the rest and bore officers' bars on the shoulder.

"I am," Red Eagle held up his flag of truce.

"Lieutenant Harding, aide to General Jackson." The young officer saluted, then frowned. "Sorry, Captain Harding. Not used to it yet."

Red Eagle led his own mule forward until he was close enough to hand the reins over. To his surprise, Harding did not order one of his men to deal with it. Instead, he climbed down from his horse and lifted McIntosh himself, before his men woke from their cold to lend him help.

"He's still alive," Red Eagle said.

"Haven't known him for long," Harding shook his head. "But he is a decent man."

"The most decent I have known."

"Will do everything we can. General Jackson is grateful for the gesture."

"My thanks for agreeing to this meeting," Red Eagle said.

Rain pattered off each of them as they transferred McIntosh to Harding's pack mule with a heave. Cold and exhausted, the men lumbered for their horses. Harding took a step back and saluted Red Eagle again.

"General Weatherford. It's been an honor."

Red Eagle hesitated before turning away.

"Tell me, Captain. Is Governor Claiborne still in the field?"

Harding paused. His eyes flickered up and down as if he were searching his memory for the proper answer.

"Governor Claiborne has been removed from his military post. He won't be on the field again."

As Red Eagle heard that all hope for vengeance was lost, he stared at McIntosh's body.

More important matters were at hand.

CHAPTER 22

The Victory Ritual

Jackson had grown tired of losing. His men were, again, in correct formation. The savages approached along the bank of the creek, concealing their numbers in the woods until, at the last minute, they popped from the trees in skirmish formation. A scattered group of Creek on the outside froze in their tracks.

"Those must be the snipers," Jackson pointed.

"Yes, sir," Captain Harding replied. "Perhaps you should dismount."

"Nonsense." A general needed to study the battlefield. The savages were only a few hundred in number. A relief, until Jackson remembered his current force was just shy of a few hundred itself. If he separated their forces, he had more chances to defeat the redskins. If his men believed they could win, he could seize momentum. He sent several squadrons to defend the three nearest forts, and sent another two on raiding parties. Fortune favors the bold, he thought. It also left him vulnerable. His best hope, once again, was training and equipment.

And strategy.

"That's it," he muttered to himself as the Indians neared. "Just a little closer…"

His eyes squinted.

"Ready…"

As they drew nearer, the sight of their war paint reminded him of the campfire the night before. He heard some militiamen, volunteers all the way from Richmond, who were convinced this land was cursed. Indian dark magic, they said. How can you kill someone, they asked, who is already dead?

"READY…"

He was waiting until he could make out the whites of their eyes. He remembered the first Indian whose eyes he ever saw on the battlefield. So black, they seemed to go forever, like death itself. A rush of chills washed up his spine.

"NOW!"

At his command, the militiamen collapsed their line back into square formations. The Indians weren't going to surprise them off the flank this time. If they could box the redskins out, they could minimize close combat and neutralize the murder in their possessed redskin eyes.

Twice more since Talladega, Red Eagle had pounced on Jackson's forces and put them to flight. If these volunteers would just hold formation, they might taste victory. If they could only know that feeling, he would have an army. He needed that mentality more than anything. He was sick of the battle being controlled by a savage.

The pop of a musket announced the starting fire. Plumes of smoke burst all around as a round ripped through the air, filling the riverbed with the fog of death. The crack of broken bones and horrible screams tested his militias. One of his men took an ax to the throat, spraying blood across the entire front line.

Just give me a shot, he thought, looking to his artillery. In the back, between formations, the big guns waited for a clean line of fire.

Red Eagle seldom gave him the shot. It was like they already knew. No, he told himself, their magic was bullshit. Then, his left flank crumbled. Men streamed back past Jackson and the guns. Screams of panic filled the air, adding to the chorus of battle cries and shrieks of agony.

"To the left!" Jackson shouted to the artillery commander. "Hit them as they pursue!"

As the commander wheeled his guns around, the right began to implode, and men started moving backward.

"Harding, whip those men into line," Jackson said.

"Yes, sir," the captain raced off to stem the tide of retreat. The boy looked like a damn soldier.

The worst of the violence was in the center, but there, his men still held. He had expected a more spirited fight after the money arrived. A volunteer doesn't desert his fellow man with cash in his pocket and bullets in his gun. Now, he just hoped they wouldn't get killed instead.

As if time considered stopping, a bullet whizzed past his head, pulling his attention to the left where he saw Red Eagle drive a leaping ax through a volunteer's skull.

Colonel Coffee galloped up between them. His head was swathed in bandages, his left arm in a splint, half of his visible flesh a mass of cuts and bruises.

"General Jackson," Coffee said. "Where would you like me?"

"Back with the doctors and the baggage," Jackson said. Coffee was lucky he couldn't see himself. "Following your orders to heal."

"Surely I can help here?" Coffee winced as a canon's roar made his horse jolt.

Jackson surveyed the battle lines.

"Fine," he said. "Ride forward into the center and take command."

"Yes, sir," Coffee saluted.

"And Coffee?"

"Sir?"

"Your command is retreat," Jackson said. "This battle is lost, save me all you can."

"How will we win," Coffee was shocked, "when all we do is retreat?"

"Retreat is not defeat," Jackson said. "It is living to fight another day."

He turned to the artillery crew.

"Do you boys have your own weapons?" he asked.

"Yes, sir," the commander said.

"Good." Jackson dismounted and drew his own sword. "This is the only line we have left, and if we don't hold it until the rest fall back, all is lost."

He turned to face the advancing Indians, the fire of war in his eyes.

"For blood!"

∽

The creek at Enotachopo was a grassland bruised, a river running red, a storm of lightning and gore. Red Eagle's latest victory had permanently altered many families for a cause that once seemed noble, but now, in the shadow of victory, it couldn't clean the water. In truth, the river didn't look of red death, but of pink sunset. Sitting on the river bank, he could only think, *It should be redder than this.*

The noise coming from Josiah and his followers spoke of slaughter. Song and dance. Stomp and chant. It rang so hollow that Red Eagle could barely think over the pit growing in his stomach. There, in the middle, Josiah made his offerings to the Breathmaker, rolling his eyes back into his head to maniacal effect.

Josiah's zealotry created a prison for Red Eagle, especially in victory. Decency and principle were held captive, and it wasn't clear if they'd ever be set free. Victory was trying to envelop him, but all Red Eagle could feel was worry.

This was only a small stretch of dirt within the infinite bounty of Mother Earth, and, until today, it was perfect. Today, it was stained by human madness. Today, river and wood were no playground. They were a prison.

With a splash, a fish leaped out to swallow a single fly, sending a squirrel running up a tree in fright. The seasons were beginning to change. Leaves would come in a few weeks, and then the flowers. This had always been Sapoth's favorite time of the year. He wanted to enjoy it for her, but the war stole his attention once more.

"Chief." Little Warrior appeared beside him. Folding in his long legs, he too settled on the ground.

"What is the count?" Red Eagle asked.

"Ninety-eight of ours dead and two missing," Little Warrior said. "Twice that injured."

"And theirs?"

"Eighteen bodies. We injured more, but their medics escaped with many of the wounded."

A roar of fury welled up inside Red Eagle. This was no victory, the cost was too great. He closed his eyes to breathe the murder from his thoughts, but all he could see was Claiborne smiling at the sight of Red Eagle's life burning to the ground. He opened his eyes and Josiah was looking straight at him. Such feelings were difficult for a leader. His was not a job to feel, but to keep other men's spirits high. He was the caretaker of his men's suffering, but who took care of his?

With a protracted breath, Red Eagle nodded his head.

"When was the last time we gained any new recruits?" he asked.

"Two months ago," Little Warrior said. "The men from Yellow Moon Creek."

"Every victory like this one only adds to Jackson's advantage. He's letting us defeat ourselves."

Red Eagle rose to his feet and walked straight for Josiah. The Corn Mother seemed to bleed between his toes with each step across the grass. He caught the eyes of Josiah and Menawa and signaled for a meeting in private. Menawa strode across the gap in a matter of seconds. Josiah felt less urgency.

"We lost five times as many men as we killed," Red Eagle said. "And you're celebrating?"

"This was a costly victory," Menawa said. "But, still, we hold the ground every time. They said Jackson would save the white man from us, yet we still haven't lost."

"It may not feel like we've lost, but we are losing. We have no new recruits. With every warrior who dies, the Creek Nation dwindles."

"No." Josiah scowled at him. "The Creek Nation remains strong. The spirits are on our side and the Americans are on the run. We have not lost yet, and we never will."

"These are nothing but petty skirmishes," Red Eagle said. "Unless we can inflict real losses on them, we will run out of warriors to hunt."

"This is feeble white man talk," said Josiah. "You forget the brothers we have lost and the brothers who still remain. You can't rob us of our victory. We won, just as the spirits foretold."

"I wish I could agree." Red Eagle took a step back. "Make arrangements for the funerals. All ninety-eight of them must be buried this evening. Tomorrow, we will have to march."

CHAPTER 23

On Holy Ground

The burden of loss lay heavy on Red Eagle's heart.

A row of Creek solemnity followed him up the winding wood hill toward the Holy Ground. They left behind hundreds of graves hastily dug by his exhausted men. Fortunate men were buried whole. Most were not. Many graves were filled with missing arms and legs, some shattered by gunfire, others discarded by the saw of survival. Red Eagle wondered how many villages were left behind, under the ground. Not enough to drive Jackson and his white soldiers from their land.

The silence was different. On the march, Josiah usually kept the warriors in a frenzy of a blood-soaked glory, but this march was different. He heard it in twilight campfires. It was the silence of reflection. From a young age, every Creek brave was taught reverence for the Holy Ground.

"Do you think that faith is rational?" Red Eagle asked Menawa as they walked up the path.

"What do you mean?" Menawa asked.

"A Frenchman named Voltaire once wrote that belief in a spirit beyond ourselves must not be based in faith alone, but in rational and self-evident truth, or nothing at all."

Menawa's brow crumpled in confusion. "Everywhere I look, I see the Breathmaker and Corn Mother," he said. "I don't know Voltaire Frenchman, but he sounds like an idiot."

"He was considered among the wisest of white men," Red Eagle said. "Then again, he was talking about the Christian God."

Menawa snorted. "The white man chooses to be blind to the connection between the Breathmaker and the Corn Mother."

Red Eagle nodded.

"You are a great leader, Red Eagle, but your European books give you strange thoughts."

The gurgle and froth of the Alabama seeped through the woods off to the right. The last of the Winter rains were always the strongest, and had left the river roaring.

A gust of wind awakened a constellation of bells and beads in the trees. Offerings of sticks and string, feathers and stone hung from above their path. Some clung to life in weather-stained fatigue, but new arrivals joined them to keep the celebration of the spirits alive. This was the way of things at Econochaca, the Holy Ground.

An opening in the woods spilled out to a clear path lined by offerings. Sentries stared down from the high ground in the distance. The path leading there was treacherous, even without a warrior's warning. Just as there were no easy paths to a good life, there were no easy ways to reach the Holy Ground.

The fragrance of smoke drifted down over their ascent as a murmur of chanting seemed to lift them upward. Cresting the plateau, they were at once greeted by all those who did not fight. Women and children, the elderly and the wounded. The Red Stick Army and its family were united again, atop this hill, in makeshift shelters built for numbers and not for permanence. The dead winter grass was already wearing into mud.

Silence fell upon the scene as Red Eagle entered. Respectful bows were chased by excited gifts of food and drink. Gratitude was shown for leading them there, for keeping the Creek from death.

Red Eagle saw it differently, and when a group of youths applauded him, he ignored it altogether. Instead, he led his horse to a trough and his followers dispersed, spreading through the camp in search of a blanket of loved ones. The spark in Mary's eyes at the sight of Red Eagle brought a smile to his face.

"It was a wise choice," Josiah stepped forward to interrupt. The prophet had already ditched his war paint and donned his ceremonial robes, as if he feared they might forget. "Coming here will keep us safe."

"It was your wisdom," Red Eagle said, "that led us here."

"The wisdom came from the spirits. They will guard and guide our every move. They will fill our counsels with wisdom and vision. Our warriors will stand, invincible to the onslaught of the white man."

All Red Eagle could manage in response was a nod. He did not feel the same security in the protection of the spirits. He was responsible for all those who died. For him, security came in walls, weaponry, and numbers. They didn't have enough of any. He knew that open disagreement with Josiah would weaken his men's spirits, but an icy wind penetrated him to his veins. Drops of cold, heavy rain quickly followed and sent people all around scurrying for shelter.

"You do not believe in this place, do you?" Josiah swept an arm across the hilltop, past tents, totems, and huts of the most dedicated medicine men, to the forests below. The spiritual center of the Creek people was now the base of the Red Stick rebellion.

"I believe in this place," Red Eagle chose his words carefully. Raindrops stung his face as he walked with Josiah toward the edge of the plateau. "It is well chosen."

"For our faith or for our defense?" Josiah asked.

"As long as we are prepared," Red Eagle said, "we can hold back four times our number. If the spirits also bless us for our presence, then all the better."

"You talk like one of them. Like the world is a tool for human hands. But we are one with the spirits and one with the land. We fight for all of it. If you cannot respect that, then you should not be here."

"Do not tell me where I should not be." Red Eagle rounded on Josiah, thrusting a finger at his chest. "I lost my family to those bastards. I do not need your spirits to know what makes a good Creek man."

"How would you know what makes a Creek man? You weren't even raised by one. Grandmother Soaring Bird whipped me if I missed a step in the sacred dances."

"No, I wasn't raised by her, but I was raised by our Creek mother. I was there when the fever came through town. I was there when she died. Where were you?"

"I wish I had been there!"

"Instead, you were in the creeks, lost in your smoking visions while I buried her. I had to burn her sheets."

"Because the white man's medicine failed. I saw past those tricks. Only the spirits could send a cure."

"And instead they sent you."

"I didn't abandon the wisdom that would have saved her."

"No, you just abandoned your mother."

"You carry the white sickness in your head. It's only our traditions that keep us alive."

"I'm the one who's sick in the head?" In a rage, Red Eagle's blood thundered through his veins and he grabbed Josiah by the scruff. "I felt my wife's blood on my hands. It was still warm. My dead son was not. He was blue and cold and innocent. If you didn't spend your days in smoke-filled dreams, you might know what's worth fighting for."

A gust of cold wind swept away the hot haze of fury. Rain ran from his brow as he stared at the shocked look on Josiah's face, and Red Eagle took his hands off the prophet.

"I am sorry," Red Eagle looked around and saw Mary and a few of Josiah's followers staring at them as the growing storm soaked them through.

On the horizon, lightning flashed.

"We will hold this ground, brother," Josiah said. "It can never be the same, but all will be well again."

Red Eagle wiped the water from his eyes.

"No, this storm of spirit and steel is of your making. You, Tecumseh, and Claiborne. Wherever it goes, destruction follows. Our only hope is to save as many as we can."

"The Spanish and the British may still come," Josiah said. "When they can, they will send soldiers from Pensacola."

Red Eagle turned his head south as though he might see that slender hope marching toward them. "I will grant you, that if they come, and we hold off the Americans on this mountaintop, then maybe we can yet win."

"Place your faith in the Breathmaker, and all will be well."

"And what of faith," Red Eagle said, "in white men from Britain and Spain?"

Turning his back on Josiah, he felt shame at pummeling his brother's hope. A retreat to the Holy Ground was not a time for splintering. It was a time for togetherness and love. He looked up to see Mary approaching, her brow crumpled with concern. She felt all the weight in his world.

CHAPTER 24

Mutiny

The thunder drummed through the night with metronomic ferocity. Just when Jackson thought he was nodding off, a crash woke him again. With each breath the thunder took, a chorus of snores snuck through the rain. It wasn't until an hour before dawn when the storm finally spent itself, and Jackson was able to sleep. It would only last an hour.

It was a different thunder that awaited him in his dreams. Artillery fire. Cannons. Men to each side of him yelling, fighting, shooting, and then ripped away as if the hand of the fog was snatching them one by one. This was the truth of sleep for the general every day since they launched the campaign. Yet, he rose with the dawn. Daylight was too precious to waste. The army needed to move, needed to continue chipping away at the dwindling Indian rebellion. His losses were significant, but so were his reinforcements, and therefore his was the advantage; however, he'd be damned if he lost all those men only to let the cursed enemy regroup, recruit, and find the resources to keep the fight alive.

Casting aside his blankets, Jackson rose from his cot, pulled on his shirt and pants, and snapped his suspenders into place. In a frozen daze, he was strapping on his boots when the tent flapped open and someone stepped inside. A drizzle of rain fell behind him and, for a split second, Jackson wished Red Eagle himself had arrived to put him to rest once and for all. After his eyes adjusted, he made out a steaming cup of coffee thrust in his direction. It was Captain Harding.

"Breakfast?" Jackson asked.

"Yes, sir," Harding answered. A worthy right hand, he'd be a terrible card player. Worry showed in every line of his face.

"Out with it, man," Jackson pulled on his coat. He picked up his sword belt and strapped it on.

"The cooks say there will be even less than the past few days," Harding said. "The supplies we received were spoiled upon arrival."

"I should have killed Claiborne when I had the chance." Jackson pounded his fist against the central pole of the tent, making the canvas shudder. "How many more days can we get through like this?"

"If we make it through one then we'll be doing well."

They emerged from the tent, the tin cup in Jackson's hand.

"Bugler!" he shouted. "It's time."

Battered brass rang out through the camp. Nothing about this scene was lively. Men staggered from their tents while others pissed by the river. Few stood at attention. Instead, a crowd faced the general.

"What's this?" Jackson snapped. "Get into line."

"No, sir." A man with a bushy black beard emerged from the front of the mob. Arms folded, he stood staring defiantly at Jackson. "Don't reckon we will."

"You are soldiers and I am your general," Jackson kept

his tone firm, but a muscle twitched at the corner of his jaw. "Step in line or face the consequences."

"We're starving. Tired. Freezing." The bearded private glared at Jackson. Behind him, men angrily expressed their agreement. "We're going home."

"No, you're not. Harding, get my riding crop."

The ground squelching beneath his feet, Harding hustled into the general's tent and handed it to Jackson. The whip in hand, Jackson strode across the camp, straight to the black beard, before yanking his jacket open, scattering his buttons everywhere.

The black beard didn't resist. He just stared at Jackson with leaden, passionless resentment. Jackson shoved him around and tore open his shirt, exposing his sinewy back.

"Punishment for mutiny is the lash." Without hesitation, he swung the riding crop with all his might. There was a crack as it hit flesh. The man winced but didn't cry out. Four more times Jackson hit him. "Are you leaving your post? Deserting the fight for freedom?"

"I am," the man gritted his teeth. "I ain't hitting no general. But I ain't marching another damn mile for the sumbitch, neither."

"You dishonor your army and your nation," Jackson's eyes boiled in the face of pacifist resistance. "I challenge you to a duel." He drew his sword and waved it at the rebellious mob. "I challenge every one of you cowards to a duel!"

Some stepped away, but most stood their ground, unmoved by the general's threat.

"I don't accept," the black beard pulled up the tattered remnants of his shirt. Reaching down into a puddle, he picked up his muddy jacket, shook it off, and pulled it on one soggy sleeve at a time, not even pausing to wince. "Nor do any of these boys. It's a losing fight. We ain't dumb enough to do that, and you ain't dumb enough to kill us if we don't. Right, boys?"

The mob stood their ground.

"You dare call yourselves soldiers!" Jackson shouted. "You dare call yourselves Americans?"

"Don't care what you call me," the bearded man replied. "But we ain't answering to no fools. C'mon, boys."

With a wave of a hand, he started for the riverside trail out of camp, the mob following in his wake. Even those who hesitated for a moment hustled to follow suit. By the end of it, half the army was marching home. And Jackson let them go.

"Dammit," Jackson said under his breath, watching the exodus. Deserters were barely better than Indians. Hell, they might even be worse. "Captain Harding, gather the officers. It's time for a new plan."

~

The distant sound of fife and drum announced the arrival of Jackson's army to Mobile, but the column of mud-stained men marching behind Jackson were not given a hero's welcome. The citizens of Mobile seemed confused. Some people stood in the streets waving and cheering, assuming victory had arrived. Others weren't so sure. Word had reached town of loss and failure. The eyes watching from the windows wanted to know why the general was here and not fighting the Indians. Surely, they hadn't lost.

"Attention!" Jackson called his men to a halt in the center

of town. Those who remained held their heads high, maintaining the illusion of discipline even in battered equipment. In spite of it all, Jackson felt pride at what they had achieved, and affection for the men who fought with him.

Harding and Coffee appeared by his side, their horses pawing the road. The young men saluted smartly, the captain still with the fresh-face and enthusiasm of youth, the colonel wearing the sardonic grin of a man who had been here before.

"Colonel Coffee, you're in charge of supplies," Jackson said. "I will sign whatever promissory notes are needed against my personal fortune, Washington be damned. Offer fair prices, don't let yourself be extorted, and don't let anyone say no."

"Yes, sir." Coffee wheeled his horse around, called a unit to follow him, and headed off down the street.

"Captain Harding, you're to find quarters for the men," Jackson said. "Empty hotel rooms, back bedrooms, barns. These people might not like it, but our boys deserve to spend a few days warm and dry."

"Yes, sir." Harding saluted and headed off.

Jackson turned to face his men.

"Gentlemen, we'll have you fed and sheltered as soon as we can," he called out. "Until then, stand easy. Smoke if you got it."

As the men lowered their guns and reached for their pipes, Jackson headed for the post office. He tied his horse up beneath a sign in the shape of a letter and headed inside.

The gray-haired woman behind the counter was genial, but completely deaf in one ear. Her desk faced the window, leaving Jackson to sit toward her side to dictate.

"To the Governor of Tennessee," he started.

"I'm sorry?" she answered.

"To the Governor of Tennessee."

"I'm sorry, hon, I'm a bit hard of hearing in this ear, can you speak up?"

"To the Governor of Tennessee."

"The government of them I see. Who is them?"

"TO THE GOVERNOR OF TENNESSEE."

"Oh, the government of Tennessee. You sure you don't mean the Governor?"

Jackson stood, picked up his chair, and moved it to the other side of her desk.

"To the Governor of Tennessee."

"Yes, dear. To the Governor of Tennessee."

"From General Andrew Jackson, currently quartered in Mobile.

"Dear Sir, I write to you in desperate need of aid. Our campaign against the natives is on the verge of victory, yet is now in danger of total collapse. The men are brave but few, their boots worn, their bellies empty. We have neither the supplies nor the troops to win. I seek your help..."

CHAPTER 25

Visions of the Future

"I saw them with my own eyes," a sly grin curling up Little Warrior's face. "Half the Americans have gone. The rest have retreated to Mobile."

Red Eagle looked around the circle at the elders and rebel leaders. Though the days were lengthening, each man was wrapped in layers of fur and hide. It was cold up here on the Holy Ground. Red Eagle gazed across the woods and creeks below. Was it his imagination or were the first green shoots appearing on the trees?

"If they cannot stand this fight," he said, as quietly as hope would allow, "then we won't need to destroy them—just outlast them."

Setting up camp here had given them hope. Days were spent walking among his followers, bolstering their spirits with talk of their strategic advantage, of holding back the American tide. Now, for the first time in months, he believed what he said.

"All thanks to Red Eagle," Menawa grinned and slapped his hulking hand on Little Warrior's shoulder, nearly knocking him over. "Victory will be ours!"

The members of the council cheered. Broken Tree and another elder exchanged nods.

On the far side of the circle, Josiah's eyes rolled back in his head. Quickly, his whole body shook, beads and feathers rattling at his wrists.

"The spirits are upon him," Menawa's eyes grew large.

Red Eagle watched his half-brother tremble as if out of control. These days, whenever praise found its way to Red Eagle, the spirits found their way to Josiah. Was it the Breathmaker who stirred his half-brother, or the drunk ambition of jealousy?

At last, the rattle of Josiah's beads slowed to a stop and his eyes came back to Earth. He slumped wearily against Menawa. Panting like a dog, he looked around the circle.

"The spirits have spoken," he said. "Our enemies are in disarray. We must seize this moment. We must attack Mobile."

Menawa's grin grew even wider. "An opportunity to finish them off."

"If half are gone and the rest exhausted," Broken Tree said, "then we can scatter them. The time has come to take Mobile."

Little Warrior's expression held a predatory gleam. "The cowards have left them, so they must feel safe. They fill their bellies and huddle under their blankets. We can pick them off as they rest."

"Summon the braves," Josiah said. "Prepare them to—"

"No."

Every face turned to see the voice of dissonance. Red Eagle lifted his head and stared right back.

Fanatics surrounded him. These were eager faces that smelled blood. Josiah stared daggers at Red Eagle, furious to find himself once again denied. The winter winds, Red Eagle feared, had blown away their wisdom. "If we strike now, it will destroy us."

"You say that the spirits are wrong?" accused Josiah. "I have been given a vision of the future."

"I say we must think before we act," Red Eagle replied. "And I, too, have a vision of the future, one born from years of experience and the entirety of this war. I have seen what it means to attack a city. They are tired, yes, but Jackson still commands them, right?"

"Yes," Little Warrior replied.

"I see us running through the streets while men fire from the cover of buildings. I see us gunned down as we burst into houses. I see artillery wheeled out to the streets, ending our warriors before we even approach our goals.

"Without Spain and Britain, the losses will all be ours. We may catch them by surprise, but then what? There are not enough of us to hold Mobile while defending our lands, and Jackson will flee with news that no city is safe from the Creek rebellion, and fear will replace the men that just deserted him. We must not stir the hornet's nest."

"If we do not act, then we are doomed," Menawa said. "Look at us. Count the men remaining. We have to act while we still have the strength to do so. With the guidance of the spirits, we can strike the winning blow."

"The spirits told us we would win our other battles," Red Eagle said. "They did not tell us the price."

A tense silence fell. The wind snatched at their hair and

shook the trees below the plateau. Among the tents, men sparred and sharpened their weapons, eager to end this long, cold wait. Some sensed a commotion among the leaders and drew near to listen.

"We are attacking Mobile," Josiah said.

"Come with us," Menawa added. "Lead us."

"No." Red Eagle held his head high. "I will not lead our people to the slaughter."

Little Warrior and Menawa exchanged a nervous look. A growing crowd of Creeks watched.

"We need you," Little Warrior said.

"I will not sacrifice that faith in me to appease this council," Red Eagle said.

Broken Tree raised a wrinkled hand.

"To attack Mobile would be bold. To do it without Red Eagle would be madness. I will not agree to this."

He stepped back and left the circle, his verdict complete.

"Look what you are doing," Josiah's eyes were two angry, glaring dots on a face creased with rage.

"With respect to Red Eagle," Menawa said, "we can do this ourselves."

Little Warrior shook his head. "Every victory was different, but every time, Red Eagle led us. Without him, I see no victory, no matter what the spirits say."

He stepped back from the circle and stood beside Red Eagle, facing Josiah across the empty patch of dirt that separated the two brothers.

"I believe in your visions," Menawa looked at Josiah, "and my heart believes in the cause. But my ax believes in Red Eagle."

The mountain of a man joined Little Warrior at Red Eagle's side. One by one, the other war leaders followed suit.

"Fools," Josiah's his face growing red with venom. "Was all the blood we spilled worth nothing? You cast aside the spirits in favor of a half-breed?"

People in the crowd gasped at Josiah's words, but none of the leaders were moved. All stood, arms folded, at Red Eagle's side, their decisions made.

Josiah glanced around in embarrassment. Half the camp had gathered to watch his shame. It made him furious. Red Eagle looked like he felt sorry for Josiah, losing face like this in front of their whole tribe. The sympathy only made it worse.

"The Breathmaker has made its will known," Josiah screamed. "Through Tecumseh. Through Tenskwatawa. Through me. How dare you stand in our way!"

"I stand for our people," Red Eagle said. "For their lives. Their future. For our lands. Nothing else matters."

"The spirit is our people. The spirit is our future. And if you stand in its way one more time, then, by all the power of the spirits, I will curse you, Red Eagle. I will make your soul shrivel and wither your life to nothing. You will be a ghost, roaming the lands of the dead."

Amid the horrified gasps of the crowd, Red Eagle stared at his half-brother. His anger was not gone, but he had no mind to unleash it now. No need. The argument was won.

"Dear brother, you forget. I am already a ghost of the husband I was. A ghost of the friend I was. The merchant I was. The man I was. You can curse your own blood if you wish, but my counsel will not be swayed by fear. I will not attack

Mobile."

With his final word, he turned his back and made for his tent. Soon, only Josiah's seething remained.

CHAPTER 26

Broken Spirits

A howl of wind tore through the trees. What charms and banners once hung in serenity were whipped into a frenzy like a bird flying before a hurricane. As the gust bit across the Holy Ground, a tremor rippled through the village of tents. A swirl of leaves rose from the ground before falling back to earth.

The sacred place had grown into a full town. Countless feet had paved mud streets between clusters of huts and a central marketplace. A collection of huts on the edge were home to Josiah and his endless ceremonies, dances, and prayers. They were filled with his followers and their glares.

Red Eagle avoided that end of camp.

Walking with slow purpose around the hill, he surveyed the Holy Ground's defenses. Fences and barricades would conceal men from the eyes of enemy soldiers, though they wouldn't last once the shooting started. He needed a proper palisade, but that wouldn't be possible until the weather became drier, and they'd need to source the timber from up the river. Perhaps he should make the arrangements now while he had the time. The biggest hurdle would be to get the warriors to agree to the work. With Josiah here, he couldn't assume anything.

As he passed each lookout, Red Eagle nodded and thanked his sentries by name. These were the quiet warriors willing to undertake a thankless but vital duty rather than ride out for glory by raiding white settlements. These were the warriors he knew he could trust, the ones who placed the tribe's good first. But it was all he could do to keep Josiah's hotheads occupied with small raids, rather than get themselves killed attacking a city.

A rider burst out of the woods below and up the winding path that led to the Holy Ground. He was driving his horse like he was trying to make its heart explode, foam dripping from its mouth. His expression, which became clear as he rode closer, was grim. Did the clouds just now darken?

Without a word, Red Eagle made for the entrance.

The rider raced in through the open gateway, glancing to see Red Eagle as he passed. He yanked on the reins, pulling his exhausted horse to a stop, before dismounting and kneeling before Red Eagle.

"Nobody kneels to me," Red Eagle urged the man to his feet. "Tell me why you've almost killed your horse."

"Out of the north," the young man nodded wildly. "The rebellion around the Lakes has collapsed. Tecumseh is dead. The Red Stick confederacy is falling apart."

Red Eagle sighed. His head sank. He had hoped that more would come of the great chief's rebellion, but he was not surprised that it had failed. Like so many, Tecumseh was driven by a fire that consumed everything around it. But like all fires, it couldn't last forever.

To Red Eagle's chagrin, others had heard what the messenger said. Before he could even respond, word whipped through the camp like a hurricane of whispers, shouts, and even wails.

A darkness descended over the Holy Ground. Now everyone felt Red Eagle's despair.

∼

"I admire your courage, Harding," Colonel Coffee tossed two pennies into the pot and revealed his cards. "But if you're ever to be a strategist, you'll have to learn to bluff."

Across the table in the Mobile drawing room, Harding let out a sigh and dropped his own cards. Grinning, Coffee dragged the pile of pennies across the table while Harding got to work shuffling the cards for more punishment. Another officer abandoned his book to join the game.

"No offense, Colonel," Harding said, "but when I want lessons in war, I won't ask the man who got himself shot."

"Battle wounds," Coffee pulled down his collar to reveal a web of pale ridged flesh. More showed beneath the line of his dark, floppy hair. "Mark of a real soldier. Ain't that right, Hickory?"

Reclining on the sofa with a cigar between his lips, Jackson smiled.

"Something like that," the general answered with a smile.

"Especially when you're too slow to get out of the way," Harding added.

"Ah, hell," Coffee said. "Deal the cards, pretty boy."

Jackson couldn't remember the last time spirits were so high. He also couldn't remember the last night he slept so well. A feather mattress and five solid hours of sleep had him feeling young again. Were it not for those bastard deserters, they'd have ended this war and all be at home with their wives by now. But as it was, they were rested and jovial, and the day off to rest their brains would suffice for now. Settling into the sofa, his gaze found the painting over the fireplace. A Dutch landscape, he figured.

A knock sounded through the door.

"Enter!" Jackson said.

The door creaked open and a grizzled militia sergeant stepped in. He saluted Jackson, who returned the gesture without rising from his seat.

"Pardon me, General," the sergeant held out a newspaper. "A boat arrived just before the hour, bringing news and letters. We're still sorting through the post, but I thought you'd want to see this."

"Schaffer, isn't it?" Jackson asked, looking the man in the eye as he took the newspaper.

The man nodded, trying to hide a smile behind soldierly professionalism.

"I remember you finding me in that dreadful hotel bar to volunteer," Jackson said. "Didn't realize you'd been promoted. Congratulations."

"Colonel Coffee's doing, sir," Schaffer replied.

"Balderdash!" Coffee called out. "I'm not the one who held that line together, Schaffer. Take some pride, man!"

"Yes, sir." Schaffer's grin was unmistakable now.

"Well, thank you, Sergeant Schaffer." Jackson glanced down at the headlines on the newspaper, then leaped to his feet. "Sergeant, could you please excuse us? And fetch me a runner. I'll need one shortly."

"Yes, sir." Schaffer saluted and turned to leave.

"Oh, and Schaffer?" Jackson waved the newspaper. "Your instinct was right. I did want to see this."

As the door closed behind the sergeant, every gaze in the room settled on Jackson, save for Coffee, who peeked at Harding's cards. The general straightened the newspaper with a theatrical snap, then held it out in front of him as he started to read.

"The headline reads: Tecumseh Dead. Is This the End of the Rebellion?" He had to wave for silence to continue. "The rebel Indian Tecumseh, who for so long has blighted communities around the Great Lakes, was finally brought to justice last Friday by General William Henry Harrison—damn, now that coot Harrison's going to think he's a huckleberry above a persimmon—in a fierce battle by the banks of the Thames River. Without their leader, the savage rebellion is on the run and in tatters. A statement from Washington indicates that... blah blah blah, congress, president, medals, and whiskey for all."

Laughter filled the drawing room.

"Gentlemen, the northern rebellion is over," Jackson said. "As I've said time and time again, the only good Indian is a dead one. Seems to me that this is the time to strike. Coffee, what's the latest on Red Eagle and his dogs?"

"They're dug in at a place they call the Holy Ground," Coffee said. "Good defensive spot. Hilltop. Woods all around. Tough nut to crack."

"Harding, how are we for men?" Jackson turned to his aide.

"Low," Harding said. "Still no word on reinforcements, and Mobile is starved for volunteers. The men we got are in good spirits now they've had a rest, but they won't fill a battle line."

Jackson turned away, drawing on his cigar as his eyes once again found the painting. Peaceful fields and quiet hamlets. This was what they were fighting for, and he'd be damned if a redskin would keep him from what was rightfully his. Was it worth the risk?

Everything hung on one question—how much did this news hurt the Creek rebels? There was no way of knowing. All he could do was use what he knew about men.

"Were I one of Red Eagle's braves, I wouldn't be feeling very brave right now," Jackson turned back to face his officers. "Tecumseh's dead. The Brits are getting it from the French. The Spanish are too cowardly to get involved. No one's coming to help, and they must know it.

"Gentlemen, look around. We are fed, we are rested, and we know that we are winning. Let's make sure the men hear about this and get 'em all a stiff drink to celebrate. Tomorrow, we kill a redskin on his knees."

CHAPTER 27

Vision

Josiah's body lay on a pile of furs in his tent, his belly rising and falling with his breath, but he was not there. The ambient swirling sound signified it was time to let go of his earthly body, and he felt his consciousness exit the back of his skull. As he drifted to communion with the spirits, he was amused by the thought that though he had no use for eyes now, that did not mean he could not see.

The sound of a thousand insects buzzed as if outside his tent. It was getting closer. The blackness of the void was broken by the grey swirl of smoke which carried the voices of his people. He heard familiar voices of men, women, and children carrying on about their everyday lives until one voice began to speak of the Holy Ground's defenses.

At once, all the other voices followed suit, forming a chorus that sang the strengths of their defensive position. The voices sped up frantically, then slowed down to a crawl before a drum beat built their song to a war cry and Josiah found himself standing upon a battleground. Flanked by his fellow Creek warriors, he looked up to see a red moon the size of earth hanging above. Its eyes were mournful, but it would not look at Josiah, instead casting its gaze upon the shadowy forest before them. Josiah raised his ax high above his head, and figures began to emerge from the trees. Their pale faces were featureless, each one identical to the next. They marched in perfect unison, holding their muskets out in front of them as if their bayonets could see.

The Creek warriors roared and charged down the hill. With axes, clubs, and spears, they wiped away the blank-faced men, and returned to the hilltop. A single tear of blood dripped from the moon, leaving a black patch in its place.

Again, the sound of marching emerged from the trees. Again, the anonymous infantry tramped forward, and again the Creek braves destroyed them. When they returned to the hilltop, Josiah saw a few of their own were lost. The moon cried another crimson tear, and again was left with another black patch.

Each time, the white soldiers advanced and were crushed by the Creeks. Each time, the moon shed a single crimson tear. Each time, Josiah strode back to the summit triumphant, the blood of his foes on his weapon.

On the seventh triumphant trip up the hillside, he found himself alone, shrouded in darkness. Everyone else was killed in the fighting. The moon was enveloped in black. Once again, the sound of marching echoed through the forest, and he knew with terrible certainty that this time he would die. The vision blew away like dust in the wind.

In the thick air of his tent, Josiah opened his eyes and stared into the fire, considering the vision the spirits had sent him. Seven times the moon had shed a tear before vanishing in the night. Seven nights of victory, after which there was only death.

How many night raids had they carried out? He could not remember, but he knew with certainty that if they didn't act now, they would be crushed by the white menace.

Leaping to his feet, Josiah snatched up his ax, pushed open the flap of his tent, and emerged into daylight. Striding to the center of the Holy Ground, he found a barrel standing in an open space and leaped atop it.

"Brothers and sisters!" He raised his ax high, his breath frosting as he called out. Many faces turned toward him. "I have a final message from the Breathmaker."

An excited murmur rippled through the camp like a pebble in a pond. The village gathered around him, their eyes finding his in anticipation. Red Eagle and the doubters stayed in the back.

"The end of the war is near," Josiah's heart swelled at the sight of so many eager warriors. "The spirits have spoken. The white men are coming, but we must not cower behind our defenses. The spirits have told me that we must attack now, or destruction will find us."

He pointed out across the crowd with his ax.

"We have seven nights to destroy the invaders. One week to soak this land with their blood. They will continue to march, but we will slaughter them as they have slaughtered our people."

Angry cries of agreement filled the air. More axes and clubs were raised.

"When they come, we will take the fight to them," Josiah continued. "We will show them the meaning of courage. As the spirits declare, victory will be ours!"

Cheers filled the camp. Someone fired a gun into the air, and others followed suit.

"Please!" Red Eagle raised his hands as he shouldered his way through the crowd. "This is madness. We should—"

"They're here!" a voice cried out from the edge of the plateau.

Leaping from his barrel, Josiah sprinted to where the sentry pointed downhill.

Ragged rows of men marched out of the woods, their muskets shouldered. Frozen clouds of breath shot out from their faces like warning fire. Trying to warm themselves, they stamped and pawed at the ground like frightened foals. Slowly, they formed lines at the command of men on horseback. The white man's officers looked down upon those they led rather than joining them in the fight like true warriors.

One of those officers looked straight up at Josiah. His was the most elaborate coat, his the best looking horse. Tall and lean, this was the first good look Josiah got of him. His angular face looked similar to Red Eagle's, and the fire in Josiah burned hotter than he knew possible.

"Jackson," Josiah seethed.

The spirits showed him the truth. If he could just take out Jackson, then surely the tables would turn.

"They have us surrounded," Red Eagle appeared beside Josiah.

Menawa was at his shoulder. He awaited instruction, but the bloodlust was on the big warrior's face. He looked to Josiah with eagerness, to Red Eagle with uncertainty.

"The militia surrounds us on three sides, the river on the fourth," Red Eagle continued. "We must look to our defenses while we consider options. Little Warrior, have the men with the sharpest eyes evaluate their numbers and quality. Menawa, gather the chiefs and wise men. We must—"

"The spirits have spoken," Josiah exclaimed for all to hear. "They have promised us victory if we are bold. Let us take this war to the white men. Let us sweep them from our land!"

Red Eagle, his face as cold and craggy as stone, reached out to grab Josiah. He twisted free and, with a loud whoop, leaped over the spiked fence defending the hilltop. Lengthening his stride, he loped toward the startled enemy. It was too late for anyone to stop the mad prophet.

Others followed, echoing his battle cry until they shook the treetops. Hundreds of feet rumbled across the dirt in pursuit. They ran without fear. They ran like braves. But as Red Eagle feared, they ran without caution, without discipline. This was not how war was won.

Josiah's heart soared as the nearest warriors overtook him. He could see their battle cry pummel the enemy as they ran. The white men were frightened, like corn before an angry scythe.

Muskets roared. War it was.

CHAPTER 28

Taking Flight

Perched atop a hill, the Holy Ground allowed Red Eagle to survey the landscape in every direction. Their position was defensive, and with their dwindling numbers, it was their best chance at survival. Perhaps, it was their only chance at all. He watched as his brave men raced foolishly down the hill, away from their defenses, and a great horror washed over him. He yelled at his men to stop their advance, but so great was his sense of dread that even he could not hear his own scream. Instead, the pit in his stomach threatened to swallow him whole.

Josiah had gotten his wish. Tact and order had lost the battle to madness. The Creek charge was wild, aggressive, and, above all, foolhardy. His spirits had driven him beyond self-destruction to sacrifice all their men, and with them, all their hope, too.

The well-practiced American gun line was ready, launching a first volley into the charging braves. Some fell. Others stumbled, but continued their advance in a trail of blood. Jackson's disciplined army stepped from the trees, as a second tier of muskets fired while the front line lowered their muskets to hastily reload.

Frantic, Red Eagle scanned around him. Not all his warriors had charged. Josiah's impulsiveness left Red Eagle with the cold assumption that all who had charged were already dead. Indeed, his only hope was to save the situation with the men who remained. Discipline and order. He turned to his side.

"Menawa, I need you to—" he started, but Menawa was gone. He glanced back downhill and Red Eagle saw the giant warrior charging alongside the other impulsive braves, club swinging around his head, long hair bouncing in the wind.

"Well?" Little Warrior asked.

At least Little Warrior could be relied upon. He stood beside Red Eagle, musket ready, with three other sharp-shooting trackers behind him.

"We have already lost," Red Eagle said. "But we can buy time for the young and old to escape. Hold the gateway, and shoot anyone who comes too close. Aim for the officers. Hold them off as long as you can."

Little Warrior nodded and turned to go.

"One more thing." Red Eagle laid a hand on his friend's shoulder. "Once they're close, get out. You are too valuable for us to lose."

Little Warrior turned with a slight smile. "The same goes for you."

Then he was gone.

The village atop the Holy Ground erupted in chaos. Women tugged children by the arm in every direction. Elders scampered quickly enough to break their bones. The reluctant grabbed their weapons and headed for the fight. One mother moved her children toward the steep descent to the river. This was the only possible escape, and the move led a tidal wave of others to follow suit. For an instant, Red Eagle felt relief that their orchestrated escape was going to plan. At least one thing was going right.

Out of the corner of his eye, Red Eagle caught a still glimpse of light brown hair amid the mayhem. Watchful and patient, it was Mary Stiggins looking directly at him. He hurried to take her by the arm.

"Josiah?" she raised a single eyebrow while looking at the men rushing at the enemy.

"Madness has ruined us," he said. "Let's get you to safety."

"Me?" Mary didn't stop him from dragging her toward the river, but her tone was indignant. "What about *you*?"

Red Eagle led her down a zig-zagging pathway from the hilltop to the riverside. Twice, the ground gave way beneath him, cascading stones down the hill to splash into the water, but each time, he caught himself.

At last they reached the narrow, stony shoreline. Three canoes sat on the shingle. Taking hold of the smallest, Red Eagle pushed it afloat and helped Mary climb in.

"Go back to your people," Red Eagle said. "You will be safe there."

"What about you?" she asked.

"My people are dying. I must be with them."

"And die with them?"

"If the spirits will it."

"To hell with the spirits."

Mary grabbed him by the collar and yanked his head down until their lips were pressed together. For a moment, the frozen battleground above vanished and the only thing that existed was her warmth joining his.

"You're the best man on that mountain," Mary whispered.

She kissed the startled warrior once more, then let go and pushed out onto the river.

"May the best man win."

He held her gaze for what might be the last moment, before thundering up the trail into camp, shouting encouragement to passing women and children streaming toward the shore.

The sound of gunfire had grown louder in his absence. The smarter braves held defensive positions and fired guns as planned. But there were not enough left. When Red Eagle reached a clear vantage point, Jackson's men had fully emerged from the woods. It would not be long before they overwhelmed his side.

Red Eagle's gray horse stood where he had left her, tied up outside his hut. Her eyes were wide in alarm, but she would not move without Red Eagle. He climbed in the saddle, ax in hand, and galloped toward the fight.

Reaching the gate, he looked down to a miserable fate. The Creek warriors unleashed vicious bravery on the enemy, but it was not enough. They had no order, no leadership. Josiah was too busy drawing blood to take command. No man's storm was vicious enough to break an entire rank of American militiamen. For every skull cracked by an ax, for every wet thud of a shattered face, his warriors turned to be stuck by patient bayonets. The war machine on the flanks fired volley after disciplined volley, advancing to envelop the natives and surround them.

Courage was never enough.

Little Warrior and his men were at the gate. They fired swiftly and accurately, picking off man after man.

"Fire there," Red Eagle pointed to the Americans' right flank. "Make an opening and we'll save who we can."

Red Eagle kicked his horse into high gear, hoping to the Breathmaker that Little Warrior had heard him. There was no time to make sure.

He crashed into the American right flank, his steed knocking two men aside as he split open another's skull with his ax.

"Out!" he shouted to the nearest braves. "You're surrounded. Get out while you can!"

Shaken into reality, even the most fanatic braves relented and pressed for the gap Red Eagle opened, retreating toward the river.

"Out!" Red Eagle yelled again, galloping into the heart of the fight. Some of their men fled in panic, heading instead for the trees, only to be cut down by the Americans.

Pressing on, Red Eagle broke through a line of Americans on the other side, but this time, he did not reach his own men. Instead, he found himself facing a ring of militiamen, all with their weapons leveled at him.

Turning in circles, he looked for a way out. The Americans were thinnest back the way he had come, for they had reached the gate by now and were advancing where his scouts had fled as ordered. If he was to get out at all, that was the only way.

With a shout, he kicked his horse into high gear once more. She jerked forward, her hoof taking a frightened soldier's face to the ground and crushing it before he could raise his bayonet. Another man leaped clear as they gathered speed toward the path up the hilltop. Guns cracked and musket balls flew from the muskets of soldiers hungry for the glory of taking down Red Eagle, but each one missed. He was thankful the fools didn't aim for his horse.

Dashing through the gate, he caught American soldiers from behind by surprise.

"After him!" a voice cried out, and Red Eagle saw the young Captain Harding frantically trying to stop his escape.

With one last burst of speed, Red Eagle's horse carried him through the camp. The captain galloped after him, and men on foot closed in from all sides. There was no escape. Sprinting through them, Red Eagle darted for the edge of the hill between fallen tents and ramshackle huts, along the mud paths of a lost people, each step farther away from the route down to the river. The only opening was the top of the bluff that looked out above the river bend.

Red Eagle's world shrank to a point of terrified, absurd excitement. Alone with his horse in a rampage of murder, he rumbled higher and higher. Fifty yards from the head of the bluff became twenty. Then ten.

Then with a whinny and a wild whoop, they leaped.

Like an eagle, his horse took flight.

The wind sliced Red Eagle's face as he dove a hundred feet from the hilltop, hopping from the stirrups to balance on the horse's back as they fell toward the river. Before they hit, he jumped off her back into the icy water, only to bob up again, horse and rider both gasping for air.

He swam for his horse, finding her reins, and led her toward the far bank.

Behind him, Captain Harding sat astride his own horse on the edge of the bluff, shaking his head in utter amazement.

CHAPTER 29

Wounded

It had been three days since the Americans decimated the Holy Ground. On the back of his horse, Red Eagle had tricked the Americans away from the Muscogee retreat, baiting them with tracks they wouldn't catch. Given the circumstances, his wounds, limited to minor scrapes and cuts, were fortunate and were beginning to scab over.

    He rode to the place his people called Tohopeka, which was where he had called his tribe to set up camp in the event of a retreat. Like his wounds, Tohopeka was scabbed by the name the white men gave it: Horseshoe Bend. To the most vehement Creek, it would only ever be Tohopeka. *Perhaps*, Red Eagle thought, *it wasn't meant to be*. Much as he had lived alongside the white man and had traded with them, perhaps the two names could never co-exist. Or perhaps, like Red Eagle, a place could exist in harmony with two names.

    For the third day in a row, Red Eagle rose just before dusk, but on this day, he would arrive at Tohopeka and examine the remains of his people. With the sun low in the sky, the trees cast dense shadows upon the river which swirled and foamed around the rocky bend. For three days, relentless rain had pummeled the lands, soaking everything under the sky. Here, the waterway thrashed anything that dared attempt to cross. While some might view it as punishment for their failings, Red Eagle recognized it as a reminder of why he had chosen this place to camp. It was their best chance at defense.

A dozen men followed behind him. All were wet, muddy, and utterly disheveled. All but one were injured. One had a fever that made his skin blaze with heat and fixed his eyes in a wide stare at the world. The yellow pus oozing from the bullet wound in his shoulder suggested he had two more nights before the walls of death closed in on him. If he was lucky, he'd die before then.

A pair of muskets sprang from bushes. Sentries raised a challenge. Camp was approaching. He had made it after all. Red Eagle was relieved that the careful necessities of real warfare had replaced the reckless abandon from the Holy Ground.

Red Eagle tipped back the broad-brimmed hat that kept the rain from his face. Recognizing their leader, the sentries lowered their guns and let the sullen procession through.

Beyond the sentry line was a fresh clearing of mud and tree stumps. Behind that, the humble beginnings of a fort. Nothing more than a solid wooden palisade interrupted by a single gate, it would not have qualified for a fort to the white men, but for them, here and now, it was everything.

The space inside the fort was far tighter than the Holy Ground. Even with their numbers depleted, tents filled every corner of the space. No one dared to pitch their home outside the shelter, and by the look of their faces, no one dared disobey Red Eagle's commands, either.

Red Eagle was stopped just inside the gate by those who had been searching for stragglers. The men and women he found along the way trudged on into the camp, bowing their heads in gratitude as they passed.

Menawa stood rigid with tension, his senses scanning around him. The proud man had spent the previous nights in teary-eyed regret for his actions at the Holy Ground. With Red Eagle returned, Menawa was intent on making up for his mistakes. Word around the camp was that he had not slept, and many worried that to continue like this was to live out his death. As long as Menawa worked, and followed his instruction, Red Eagle did not care. If not for Menawa, there would be many more survivors. If he chose penance for his failings, Red Eagle wouldn't stop him.

Next to him stood Little Warrior and two of his scouting comrades. The third had been missing since the battle, and was feared dead. Calm and determined, they looked to Red Eagle for reassurance and direction.

"You should see this," Little Warrior winced. His skin was pale and he didn't so much speak as grit words through his teeth. Resentment simmered across his face in a standoff with pain. The others knew Little Warrior concealed a wound. He looked like shit, and if he waited much longer, it might be too late.

"Go to the medicine man," Red Eagle said.

Little Warrior ignored the remark and gestured toward a shadowy shape by the wall, which uncurled and rose into the figure of a man obscured by blankets draped over shivering shoulders. Deep, dark shadows hid his downcast eyes. His hair hung limp and disheveled down his chest. Before he could see him, Red Eagle knew the burden he carried.

"I thought you must be dead," Red Eagle said.

"I should be," Josiah replied, his voice weary.

Seeing his half-brother broken and miserable, Red Eagle had sympathy for him. There was no avoiding the truth. This was Josiah's fault. They might not have destroyed Jackson's army, but more would have survived to be sure. He wanted to reassure Josiah that all would be well, that he had done what he thought was right, and sometimes that was all a man could do.

But he knew such an olive branch would give Josiah fuel to the dying embers of his self-destructive prophecy.

"You are here now," Red Eagle said. "You must fight for your people. That is reason enough to live."

Josiah didn't respond, but slumped back down beneath his blankets. Red Eagle turned to Menawa.

"You cleared the approach."

"As you commanded," Menawa replied.

"You did well," Red Eagle offered his fellow war leader a shred of dignity. "Was there good timber?"

"Not here, but we went deeper into the woods and found it." Menawa pointed out of the gate to a pile of tree trunks at the edge of the woods.

With his fellow leaders in tow, Red Eagle walked over to inspect the logs. Not all were as straight as he would have liked but they would have to do.

"My father fought in the revolution," Red Eagle looked from the logs to the fort and then back again. "It was from him that I learned the ways of war."

"You do not fight like an American," Little Warrior said.

"For me, the world is not divided into settler and native. I am both, and I was before Claiborne and Tecumseh tore us apart. I do not pick and choose which parts to keep. A death in my family started this war, and you asked me to lead you, but not before rejecting the rest of my family, McIntosh, and other settlers who shared our way of life. Tecumseh rejected it for ambition. Josiah rejected it for the spirits. I had no choice but to reject it for my revenge. This is what happens when we reject who we are for who we want to be. The time for rejection will soon be past. We must learn acceptance, or we will never know peace."

Darkness had fallen. Burning brands were lit along the wall, illuminating the open ground before the defenses. They stood in silence, hanging on his every word. To hear their commander lay himself bare, sharing his sorrows and piling up his guilt, everyone was sent into the prison of lost causes.

"Layer the walls." Red Eagle pointed from the pile of timber to the walls of the fort. "We face European cannon, so we must have European defenses. The outer layer will absorb some of the shots and keep the main walls up for longer.

"Cut portholes all along the line. We must be able to fire from the full cover of the fort. If we have time, we will build an earth bank. It will absorb their shot better. But I doubt Jackson gives us time. He is no fool."

"As you command," Menawa waved at a band of men by the gate, then turned for the nearest of the felled tree trunks, ready to start work.

"Not now," Red Eagle laid a hand on his shoulder. "Time is short, but better to do good work rested and in the light. Sleep, my friend. Prove your strength to us tomorrow.

"All of you, rest now, but rise with the dawn. The Americans are coming and, when they do, we will show them how real warriors fight."

As the others headed back into the fort, Red Eagle drew Little Warrior aside.

"I have another task for you. Have your scouts gather every canoe within a day's walk up and down the river. Place them on the bank at the end of the bend. If these walls fall, I want our people to have a way out. My family is dead. No one else should suffer the same fate. And if you don't rest, your family will."

CHAPTER 30

A Worthy Adversary

As much as he admired the ingenuity of a good telescope, Jackson hated to use the damn things. All that squeezing one eye shut and squinting through the other was enough to give a fellow a headache. On top of that, telescopes were almost always the bearers of bad news. If you knew that a thing would go well, then you didn't need to peer through a tube to learn about it. Telescopes were there for when you needed to know how bad things had gotten, or to determine how bad they were about to be.

Today was no exception. They had found the damned Indians, after Red Eagle led them on a wild goose chase in the opposite direction. The dogs were lucky to have a leader who was half white. It almost leveled the playing field. His brow furrowed as he pressed the cold metal tube to his eye and moved it carefully around, taking in as much as he could of the rebel defenses. It was an inexact business, spying from a hilltop this far back upon the far side of the bend. He was smart to have traded safety to other redskins in exchange for their tracking. Even a savage knew a losing fight when he saw Jackson with all his weaponry, and, besides, none of the

American scouts ever made it back alive. The trees, on the other hand, were just beginning to show signs of life, sprouting with the first green shoots of spring. It was enough to block his view at this distance, but it wouldn't hide an army for long, and that was a problem.

Not as much of a problem as their defenses, though. The fortifications across the neck of the bend appeared sturdy and grew sturdier by the hour. The other three sides of the Indian camp were protected by rough and fast flowing waters. There was only one way in. Red Eagle sure was a clever bastard.

Beneath him, his horse took a step forward, looking for greener grass to nibble at.

"Gentlemen, take note," Jackson lowered the telescope and turned to his officers. "Next time some damn fool from Washington tries to lecture you on the ignorant savage, I want you to remember this. A carefully chosen site. Rapidly assembled fortifications. Savages might as well be Caesar and the Roman legions. It appears they built walls to withstand feeble artillery, and, unfortunately, that's all we've got. These dogs have cunning. Remember this, Red Eagle's one of us. A fine mind."

His horse took another step forward, still looking for something better to eat. Jackson shared her impatience at the limitations of his surroundings.

"We need someone to ride closer," he said. "Get a proper look."

For a long moment, his officers sat exchanging silent glances, eyes flitting back and forth until all settled upon the youngest. Reluctantly, Harding raised his voice.

"A better look at their defenses," Harding began, "might

also give us a better count of the warriors inside, General. But their scouts are likely to catch us and expose us all."

"I'm willing to risk it," Jackson said, a twinkle in his eye. "Where's your fighting spirit, Harding?"

"It's not the fighting I'm worried about, sir," Harding replied. "It's giving up the element of surprise."

Jackson laughed. Frustrated as he was, he was also proud of how far Harding had come. A few months ago, the kid couldn't even ride a horse, but now he knew how to manage men, including his own commander. He was one hell of an apprentice.

"Fine," Jackson said. "I have a meeting with a government man this afternoon. Wouldn't want to burden you boys with that sort of horror."

They rode from the hilltop away from Horseshoe Bend, through the green buds of spring, and toward the less fresh sounds and smells of the militia camp.

∽

"Cut the horsecrap," Jackson snapped, glaring at the suited men sitting in his tent, each of them filling one of his precious camping chairs. "I need everything you have, and I need it now."

"Really, General Jackson?" Mister Copperfield from the War Department asked. The fat bastard had put on yet another chin since Jackson saw him last. Flesh bulged over the collar of his shirt as if it was making a run for it. It was a repulsive sight. "I thought that you had the savages on the run. The country is ablaze with talk of your victory at the Holy Ground."

"I didn't win at the Holy Ground," Jackson said. "They lost."

Copperfield spluttered with laughter and shook his head. The two locals sent on behalf of the local governors followed suit, but at least their necks jiggled less.

"Coffee, please explain."

Coffee pushed away from the tent pole on which he had been leaning, a sardonic look on his lean face. His well-earned promotion to General had come through at long last, and with it an extra swagger in his step. He tapped the ash from the end of his cigar and made a point to brush aside his floppy hair before regarding the government suits like they were so many weevils trying to eat his biscuits.

"We took captives at Holy Ground. There are two factions among the rebels.

"Religious fanatics who swear allegiance to the Prophet Josiah and some invisible spirit in the sky, and the hard-headed pragmatists like William Weatherford, whom you know as Red Eagle. Holy Ground was Josiah's doing. He ran straight for us with eyes as crazy as a man in a fight with the bottle. Apparently, he told them their heathen gods would protect them, and then led his own men to the slaughter. Those men were fools, but that was some hard fighting."

"So what's the problem?" Copperfield asked, reflecting Coffee's disdain back at him. "Can't you beat fools twice?"

"The fools are gone. We killed them dead. Only ones left are Weatherford's, and his father was a European. He ain't no fool. Used tactics from Alexander the Great on us. Now he's building European defenses for a European fight.

"Make no mistake, gentlemen. Horseshoe Bend ain't no

Holy Ground. To break through them walls, we need more men, we need more guns, and we need a hell of a lot more ammunition."

"We don't need any more excuses." Copperfield stood. "Just do your job, General."

He stalked out of the tent.

As the other two bureaucrats rose, Jackson held out his hands.

"Gentlemen, Washington has failed us because, if we lose, these Indians won't go all the way up there to go berserk. Can you say the same for your states?"

"Why should we risk what they won't?" one of the men said.

"Someone will get credit for helping me bring down the largest rebellion this country has ever seen," Jackson said. "Someone will feel that glory. The press loves me. When I speak to them after we end this charade, I'm going to tell them exactly who helped me, and exactly who didn't."

The two bureaucrats glanced at each other, recognizing their colleague as competition.

Muttering hurried farewells, they rushed from the tent and headed for their horses.

Settling into one of the vacated seats, Jackson stretched his legs out and gestured for Coffee to take the seat beside him.

"That got their attention," Coffee grinned as he pulled a cigar from his pocket and handed it to Jackson.

"You think it'll work?" Jackson asked.

"Depends on how unpopular raising fresh militias makes them, but I'm hopeful."

Jackson moved across the tent for his writing desk, examining the map spread across it. They knew all about Weatherford's defenses—how they were placed, how they were built, where they seemed strongest. None of that information was complete, but even so, it showed how capable this opponent was. The brutal savage he heard about from Fort Mims was an adversary worthy of respect.

"We need more intelligence," he said. "Send our three fastest riders to where William Weatherford grew up. Tell them to talk with neighbors, business associates, anyone they can find. I want to know more about who he is, where he comes from, how he thinks and why."

"I could try asking the prisoners," Coffee's cigar smoke seeping out with each word. "Some of them might know him well."

"That too," Jackson said. "Find out everything from everyone. In three days' time, bring it all to me."

CHAPTER 31

The Terms

Militiamen marched in neat columns into Jackson's camp. It was the second group to arrive that day, and Harding ushered them to the opposite side of the field to set up their camp. Their officers looked in annoyance at those of the other regiment, who smiled and waved, safe in the knowledge that they had won the race to aid General Jackson.

The general himself was feeling magnanimous, and he looked it, too. Sitting in a chair atop a hill overlooking the camp, he penned a letter to the newspapers back home, telling how both governors had come through for him. Credit where credit was due.

With a smirk, he lamented the War Department's absence. That should send Mister Copperfield and his chins scrambling.

Coffee strode up the slope toward Jackson, a steaming tin cup in each hand.

"Here you go, General," he held a cup out to Jackson. "My namesake."

"So they've invented a drink called 'general' now?" Jackson asked. The metal cup almost burned his fingers as he took it. He was glad of the warmth but would be gladder still to be home with his wife's china, let alone a flavor other than burnt.

He took a sip and raised his eyebrows in surprise. It was actually rather good.

"Harding again," Coffee saw Jackson's expression. "No end to the man's talents."

"He'll be a general soon at this rate," Jackson said.

"President even," Coffee replied.

They drank their coffee and Jackson finished his letter, carefully sealing it for delivery. As he cleaned his pen and stoppered the ink bottle, the last of the militia tents were going up.

"Will this be enough?" Coffee asked. "To end this war, I mean."

"I think so. There can't be more than a thousand rebels inside that fort and not all of them are warriors. We have five times that, plus artillery."

"Good," Coffee's expression was unusually serious. "We carry on like this much longer, I might get a taste for it."

"And here I was thinking you were a true soldier," Jackson studied his subordinate's face.

Coffee's hand went, apparently without thought, toward his scars. "I take my job seriously, but I'm more than a soldier."

Jackson pondered those words. He felt the same about himself, yet here he was, leading one military campaign after another. Was he just a soldier? Did he want to be more?

"Excuse me, General Jackson, sir." Captain Harding saluted as he approached. "There's someone here I think you should meet."

Beside Harding stood a hearty woman with red cheeks and light brown hair. Even in a weather-worn dress with mud around the hem and a faded traveling cloak, she carried herself with an easy grace.

Realizing that they were in the presence of a lady, gentlemanly habits caught up with Jackson and Coffee. Both men lurched to their feet.

"General Jackson, this is Mrs. Mary Stiggins," Harding said. "Mrs. Stiggins, this is General Jackson, commander of this expedition, and General Coffee."

"Pleased to meet you, ma'am." Jackson lowered his head and kissed the back of Mrs. Stiggins' hand. Coffee made a bigger display of the gesture, bending one knee and twirling back his spare hand like a caricature of a French gentleman. Harding's face tilted to the side in confusion while everyone else fought to contain their laughter.

"Mrs. Stiggins is the sister-in-law of Captain McIntosh," Harding said.

The laughter died immediately.

"Your brother-in-law is one of the finest men I've ever had the pleasure of serving with. His courage, skill, and character are missed by all," Jackson said. "You'll be pleased to know he's recovering well in Mobile."

"Thank you," Mrs. Stiggins said. "This is the best news I've received in years."

"I'm sure. And how can I help you, Mrs. Stiggins? Have you come seeking McIntosh?"

"No." Mrs. Stiggins shook her head. "I was a captive of the rebel Indians. Red Eagle let me go during the attack on the

Holy Ground, and I've been looking for safe shelter."

"You've found it. Captain Harding will arrange a tent for you. Will you dine with me this evening?"

"I would be honored."

"Splendid. Perhaps then you can tell me what you know about him."

∼

Long before the scouts ran back through the gates of the fort, Red Eagle knew that the Americans were marching on Horseshoe Bend. They had moved across the river days before, camping a few miles south. When they prepared to advance, every bird on that side of the woods took flight, scared away by the tramping of boots and the shouting of commands. The skies grew clear as they extinguished their fires, ending the smoke.

The time had come.

With a heavy heart, he clambered down the ladder from the guard tower beside the gate. When the first scout returned, Red Eagle was waiting for him in the gateway.

"All of them?" he asked.

The man nodded. "Less than an hour."

Red Eagle stayed in the gateway as more reports came in. The American artillery was slowed by mud and roots. That bought a little time, but the good news ended there. The scouts counted four or five thousand men, all armed with muskets, and Jackson at their head.

Little Warrior was one of the last scouts to return. He favored one leg and winced as he shifted his weight onto it. A sickly scent followed him.

"Did you not go to Josiah?" Red Eagle asked.

"Too late now," Little Warrior said. "It's time to fight."

"It is never too late to choose to live."

Little Warrior ignored him and went to take his place at the loopholes in the wall.

Red Eagle turned his head to the side, certain he heard steady murmur of marching sneaking between the trees. His heart began to pound, drowning out the marching. Was he imagining things? He closed his eyes, and listened intently. Sapoth's broken face and Claiborne's demonic smile flashed through his mind, and he whipped open his eyes.

"They're here," said Little Warrior.

At last, the Americans marched out of the woods. Columns of men peeled off to left and right, forming ranks along the tree line. Like the fortified walls, they filled the narrow bend from river bank to river bank, cutting it off from the outside world.

A lean figure on a black horse walked between the lines, pulling out a white handkerchief and waving it above his head. He trotted forward, and stopped in the middle of the clearing.

Red Eagle walked out to meet him.

"General Jackson, I presume."

"General Weatherford," Jackson saluted. "Or would you prefer Red Eagle?"

"Both names belong to me."

"It seems that my intelligence was correct," Jackson said. "You are more pragmatic than the papers give you credit for. Is there any chance you might surrender?"

"What are your terms?" Red Eagle asked. He once had

dreamt of a peaceful ending, of an end to the bloodshed.

"A complete end to the fighting. You hand over all of your weapons. This fortress, and any others like it, are dismantled. The ringleaders of your rebellion, including yourself and the so-called Prophet Josiah, will stand a fair trial for your actions. If you accept these terms, then I will plead for leniency on your behalf. All others within the fort will be allowed to go free, on the understanding that a return to rebellion will result in complete annihilation."

Red Eagle nodded. "A fair trial."

A smirk curled up Jackson's lip. They understood each other.

Red Eagle considered the offer. His freedom, probably his life, and those of a handful of others, in return for hundreds of lives. People allowed to go free despite all that they had done.

It was as good an ending as he could hope for.

"I must talk with others," Red Eagle said.

"Of course," Jackson replied. "I'll give you an hour."

One hour. The same amount of time his scouts estimated it would take for the Americans to wheel in their artillery. That sounded right.

Before Jackson turned his horse to trot away, he added, "You should know. McIntosh lives."

∽

Back inside the fort, Red Eagle gathered the warriors around him and explained Jackson's terms.

"We should take this. Otherwise, there will be only death here."

"There has been death already," Broken Tree looked as weary as everyone else, but there was a spark in his eyes. "I have lived a long life. When I was young, I fought for our people. I fought for our lands. I have seen battles with the white man, and I have seen the white man's idea of peace. They will not stop until they take everything from us, no matter what he says. There's no turning from this fight."

There was little debate. Red Eagle looked to Menawa, but his eyes were pointed downward. The Holy Ground broke him. Josiah, shamed by what he had done, could not speak, either. A vote was proposed and hands were raised.

The outcome was clear. Red Eagle walked back out through the gates and over to where General Jackson waited.

"I thank you for your offer," Red Eagle's words were heavy on his tongue, "but we choose to fight."

Jackson gave him a curious look as though he were weighing something in his mind. "Is it true?" he asked. "That you ordered the massacre at Fort Mims?"

"If your men do not listen to you, General, then what's the difference?" Red Eagle asked.

With leaden steps, he returned to the fort.

CHAPTER 32

The Walls Close In

The artillery crews saluted as Jackson trotted up to them on his horse. There were only two guns, both small enough to have been transported through the difficult terrain around the Creeks. He was putting a lot of faith in not a lot of firepower.

"Ready, gentlemen?" he asked.

"Yes, sir," the crews replied in unison.

"Fire at will," Jackson commanded.

The guns boomed, sending Jackson to the end of the line where Captain Harding was waiting. He had left his horse at camp, marching through the woods alongside the infantry to keep them in order.

"General Coffee is in place, sir," Harding said.

"Excellent. If we're lucky, we won't need him."

He watched as a cannonball hit the fort, erupting with a shower of splinters.

∽

Dust flew from the wall as another cannonball struck the outer defenses. For an hour, the Americans had pounded away, but the Creek warriors stood safe behind their defenses.

"You did well, Menawa," Red Eagle said.

"Tell that to the men at the Holy Ground. I led them to a fool's death."

Red Eagle placed a hand on the other warrior's shoulder. "I don't need your lament. I need your strength. You're the best we have, now act like it."

Red Eagle looked down the line. Creek warriors waited patiently by the loopholes, muskets loaded and ready. Others crouched behind the rampart fighting platform, axes and clubs in hand, waiting to fight any Americans who made it over. Only Little Warrior's sharpshooters were firing, and at this range, even they were finding few marks. Red Eagle found Josiah's eyes and gave him a nod. Josiah began a war chant, and so began the thunder of drums. Each bang of percussion sparked a glimpse of mayhem in Red Eagle's mind. The labored breathing of a sprint, the crack of an ax into a skull, the scream of a man who would never walk again. A boom sounded in the distance, and the whizz of the shot split through the air before it collided with the walls and sent wooden shrapnel everywhere.

A scream brought Red Eagle back into the moment as he looked to see one of his men fall from the parapet, a jagged chunk of wood embedded deep in his shoulder. A medicine man rushed to help him, yanking out the colossal sliver before pressing herbs into the wound and dressing it with a bandage.

Still the artillery continued to thunder, and still the walls held strong. The Americans would not break in this way.

∼

Creeping to the edge of the woods, General Coffee looked out across the creek. From here, the whole rebel camp lay open to him, right up to the back of their stockade. All he had to do was cross the creek with his select men. Good thing they brought help.

McIntosh's Cherokee ally, Major Ridge, crept beside Coffee, along with nearly one hundred Cherokee warriors, and a few dozen of McIntosh's Lower Creek warriors as well. They were at home among the woods and the river. They faded into the woods far better than Coffee's men.

Across the water, the Red Stick rebels focused on the artillery fire pounding against their walls. It was time for attack.

"Men," Coffee signaled to his uniforms. "Stay on the bank. Cover us as we cross."

They stepped backward, behind the line of native warriors, and took staggered positions behind the cover of trees.

Coffee turned to Major Ridge. "Now is the time to prove our alliance."

Ridge nodded to his warriors, who moved forward, silently setting canoes in the current.

McIntosh's men followed suit. Every half-dozen men carried a boat between them. Most were little more than wooden tubs taken from farms up and down the river. Three were canoes captured at the Holy Ground. One was a coracle built by militiaman from an Irish family, and three men struggled to fit inside.

Wading into the shallows, half the Americans and their allies climbed into their boats, set their paddles to the water, and rowed.

Coffee, taking his place at the front of a lead canoe, felt the vessel buck and lurch beneath him. The water was as rough as a sailor's saloon. He felt a rush of adrenaline and ached to whoop with excitement, but he knew to save it until they were detected.

Coffee looked to his left as a panicked American grabbed the gunnels of his canoe, sending all six men into the drink. He hoped the loud splash was hidden by the river's roar. To his right, the crew of another lost control and were swept away around the bend. But Ridge and his men beat a lead pace against the current. Swift and silent, they neared the exposed underbelly of the rebel camp.

A dozen yards out, a sentry on the opposite bank noticed them. Panicked cries cascaded through the Creek camp. Bullets began to fly as the rebels rushed to defend a new front.

∽

"They're behind us!" someone shouted. "They're on the river!"

Red Eagle raced through the camp, Menawa beside him. A musket ball whistled past his head as he approached the bank of the creek.

Three boats had arrived and more were on their way. Cherokee warriors leaped out, guns leveled, firing as fast as they could.

"Take half the men," Red Eagle said to Menawa. "Form a line here. We need to drive them back before—"

"The walls!" someone shouted from behind him. "They're at the walls!"

Muskets fired on both sides of the camp. Two more boats landed, their American occupants rushing out to face Menawa's hastily assembled warband. Ladders clattered against the stockade, and Jackson's men began their dangerous climb. Gun smoke filled the air.

"They will not pass," Menawa shouted. "Go command the walls!"

Hefting his ax, Red Eagle rushed back to the gateway. He ascended a ladder two rungs at a time and leaped onto the parapet as an American soldier appeared at the top of the wall. Swinging wildly, Red Eagle ripped his neck apart, his body tumbling toward the ground.

A bullet struck the defenses an inch from Red Eagle's waist. He ducked behind the timbers and waited for the next attack to come.

∼

Captain Harding raised his sword above his head. With his other hand, he carried a scaling ladder, its weight shared with half a dozen other men. He would not ask them to do this if he was not willing to do it himself.

"Forward, boys!" he waved the sword above his head.

They ran toward the fort, others running beside them. Muskets barked all around. The man behind him fell, blood pumping from his thigh, and another man took his place. His men took his command. Jackson had taught him well.

They reached the wall and mounted the ladder. All along the line, soldiers repeated the action, and it was working. With half the rebels drawn off by Coffee and Ridge, here, they had the advantage. Parts of the rampart were taken by the Americans, and they proceeded to fire down into the camp below. The fight was downhill.

Harding placed his foot on the ladder, and fear dropped his stomach. He steeled himself. That feeling would not master him. He would do General Jackson proud.

Holding his sword up in a preemptive parry, he rushed up the ladder as fast as he could.

As he reached the top, a Creek ax clanged against his sword, knocking his blade back into his forehead with a shallow cut. A good thing he held it there. But then the ax swept around. Still clinging precariously to the ladder, Harding was slow with his riposte, and the flat of the ax caught a glancing blow against the side of his head. Dizzily, he swayed on the top rung, black spots dancing across his vision. There was a crunch and a terrible rush of pain. Looking down, he saw blood spray from the mangled ruin that had been his arm.

Darkness swallowed him as he fell.

∼

One whole side of the fortifications had fallen. Pulling the musket men back from the walls, Red Eagle set them to firing at the Americans as they reached the top. It was the only chance to drive them back, and it was slim.

Muskets snapped and weapons cracked. Men screamed in pain and in rage. Somewhere, a baby was crying.

Some of the soldiers and warriors from the river had made it off the bank and into the camp. Red Eagle rushed to intercept them, a handful of braves by his side. The fighting was swift and brutal. Creek against American. Creek against Cherokee. Creek against Creek. They could not hesitate or use caution. Every moment counted. They had to kill anything that moved.

As they drove the raiders back, another cry went out to the left. Militiamen were pouring over the walls at that end.

Red Eagle ran over. There were too many Americans on the walls now to go up and face them. Instead, he ordered axes to ladders to strand them above. At least then they were sitting ducks.

Twenty yards away, Little Warrior crouched, firing up at the Americans on the walls. One man fell, then another. He was so close, it was impossible to miss.

The Americans realized it, too. Spotting Little Warrior where he crouched behind a tent, four of them turned their guns on him. The breakneck rampage of battle froze, as Red Eagle cried out for Little Warrior to take cover.

It was too late. Guns roared. Little Warrior fell, blood spurting from his mouth, as his lifeless face found the mud. One more body to the pile of hundreds lost at Horseshoe Bend.

CHAPTER 33

Scorched Earth

There was blood on Josiah's hands. So much blood. The blood of every man who fell from the walls, of every man he rushed to help. Blood of men he had saved and blood of men he could not. Blood of men who were already dead upon arrival. He tried to wipe it off, but no matter how hard he tried, he'd never wipe away the blood of those he led to the slaughter at the Holy Ground.

Had the Breathmaker deceived him or had he deceived himself? Whatever the truth, he could not trust himself to interpret the signs any longer. Could not trust the guides that led him for so long. All he could do was rush from one moment to the next, hiding from his failings in the swiftness of action.

The Creek warriors were on their heels, pressed back toward the center of the camp where the crowd of civilians screamed in terror, the women trying to shield their children from the grisly storm approaching. Now, when the wounded fell, Josiah could not reach them. American soldiers stepped on and over their bodies like Indian skin rugs. It was time for him to touch another kind of blood.

Drawing his war club, he stepped in the way of an approaching Cherokee warrior. He would not let his people die without putting up a fight. Perhaps then he could earn back the favor of the spirits, trading enemy blood for good will. He brought his club back.

The warrior's gun roared. Josiah was hurled back by the impact on his chest. The screams went silent. He lifted his head off the ground, looking to the burn in his chest. Blood spurted from a hole within him, and the taste of salt filled his mouth. He needed a drink of water. He tried to ask for one, but all that came out was a glug of blood. A rush of cold enveloped him.

The red hue of war paint, the symbol of his strength, was not noticeable now. Blood covered his body head to toe. He closed his eyes and saw the Corn Mother before him, ready to carry him away.

～

"Back to the river!" Red Eagle yelled. "Get the women and children out."

He couldn't tell how many of the warriors heard him, or how many were even left. The Americans were closing in from both sides, some coming from the riverbank, some from the wall. The thinnest line was by the river. That was his best hope. He grabbed a few men and ripped an opening for the civilians to escape. Women and youths helped the elderly and infants into canoes.

The first canoe pushed away from the bank. As it drifted into the river, an American soldier grabbed it and stop the escape. Menawa leaped upon him, cutting him down with a single blow, then pushed the canoe farther out. It was caught by the current and swept away.

Red Eagle returned his gaze to the battle and found three soldiers closing in on him. The first hesitated, but Red Eagle did not, smashing the man's arm with a chop of his ax. He crumpled to the ground, grabbing his phantom limb.

The next man lunged with his bayonet. Reflexes slowing with exhaustion, Red Eagle stepped aside a moment too late. The blade cut a shallow gash across his chest and he felt the sting of cold air on the wound as he spun to pop the man's neck with the pommel of his ax. Though he didn't bleed, he also didn't move again.

He whipped his head around for the third soldier, but he had swung his gun like a bat, and it slammed into the side of Red Eagle's head.

The world went black.

∽

Knee deep in the icy shallows, Menawa looked around to see how many more were fleeing his way. There weren't enough canoes.

A far worse prospect caught his eye. He saw the butt of a musket collide with Red Eagle's head. The war chief fell on top of a man he had just cut down, while another soldier stood over him, a triumphant look on his face.

It was as if an eagle's talon tore at Menawa's heart. Red Eagle had tried to save them. Menawa had failed his people, and now, because of him, Red Eagle had fallen, too.

He refused to fail Red Eagle again.

Running up the riverbank, Menawa hurled his ax through

the mayhem ahead of him. It tore through the air and found a satisfying stick in the soldier's ribs. The soldier dropped his gun, staggered for a few steps, and tried to yank it out, but then fell to the ground.

Sprinting his way, Menawa drew a knife from his belt and stuck it in the man's neck. He lay on the ground, twitching, and his life left him through a spurting carotid artery.

Soldiers swarmed for him from every direction. Menawa lifted Red Eagle in his arms. His leader was limp and his chest was plastered with blood. He would not let himself believe that he was too late. Musket balls hissing past, he rushed Red Eagle back into the shallows and placed him in a nearly full canoe. Pushing with all his might, he sent it down the river with the others. Fifty of the Creek people hurtled away on the rushing current.

Menawa turned to meet his fate.

∼

General Jackson rumbled through the gate, scanning the scene for Red Eagle. Fighting was contained to the shoreline, the last of the rebels unwilling to surrender, swinging their weapons until the last drop of blood was spilled. They had killed far more of his men, but they were almost spent. He would not have mercy on them today. Too much horror had come today to allow the savages any hope of starting the cycle up again. Rebellion would raise its head in these lands no more.

Watching Harding fall with his own eyes was ghastly. That young man was the best he had, his whole decorated life before him. Instead, he fell screaming from the walls in the rain of a bloodbath, his arm tumbling to the ground, never to be used again.

The enemy was so outnumbered that many of his men stood uncertain, their chests heaving as they gathered their breath. The fighting continued by the river.

"Sergeant Shaffer," Jackson called out, seeing a familiar figure rallying men by the gate, preparing them in case of a counter-attack they could all see was not coming.

„Sir," Schaffer saluted smartly.

"Take these men and look for firewood. Lamp oil too. There must be both in this camp."

"Sir?" Shaffer said uncertainly. It wasn't the sort of order one expected on the battlefield.

"I want you to set these walls on fire, Schaffer. These walls and anything else they could use against us. Collect their weapons. Burn anything that might be used against the United States of America.

"We have won, Sergeant Schaffer. Let's make damn sure we never have to do it again."

∾

The sun sank toward the horizon in a sky scorched orange. A silhouetted column of smoke wafted against it, taking with it the ghosts of Horseshoe Bend.

A mile south, Andrew Jackson stood in a clearing with Mary Stiggins. In front of them were a row of blankets, each covering a single sad form.

"I'm sorry for making you do this, ma'am. But after your captivity, you know these men better than anyone here."

"Never apologize for doing your duty, General. You do

yours and I shall do mine."

"Thank you, ma'am."

Her voice was strong, but her face held a dread that he had not expected from a woman of such character. She had survived Fort Mims, she had seen dead bodies before. Seeing her reeling, however, gave him a vile unease.

An infantryman was standing by the bodies, but Jackson brushed him aside and lifted the first blanket himself.

"These are all men singled out as leaders in the fighting. Do you know this one?"

"I know the face but not the name. I think he was from one of the northern tribes."

"This one?" Jackson lifted the next blanket.

Mary closed her eyes for a moment before speaking. "I know him. Little Warrior. The head of their scouts. He was… Well, does it matter what sort of man he was? God will judge him now."

She did not know the next face or the one after that. The fifth made her pause for a long time while wearing a strange expression, one that was not truly grief.

"That is Josiah. The Prophet. He led the most fanatical warriors."

"One of the ringleaders," Jackson said. "Good."

Mary hesitated again before letting him reveal the last face. When the blanket was torn aside her expression went from fear to relief.

"I'm sorry. I don't know him."

In his heart, Jackson had held both hope and dread that William Weatherford might be among the fallen and that he had not recognized the face of a man he had just met. He was a man of character, but he dreaded the thought that Red Eagle was alive out there somewhere. He needed the rebel Creek commander brought to heel, publicly and permanently.

"Tell General Coffee to bring his prisoners," he called out.

A soldier ran off into the woods. Two minutes later, he returned alongside Coffee, trailed by a dozen men guarding four prisoners. Three of the prisoners were old and wrinkled. They were no threat. The fourth, bloodstained and brooding, looked tough enough to take them all on.

"This is Menawa, one of the war leaders," Coffee said. "The rest are elders, men of influence in Creek councils."

"Do you have their word not to fight if we let them go?" Jackson asked.

"Our fighting is done," Menawa's voice rumbled like rocks sliding down a mountain.

"Good," Jackson said. "Then I want you to take a message to your people, wherever they are, whether they fought or not. The war is over. Tell Red Eagle he must surrender himself."

A horrible echo of Harding's scream bolted Jackson with a sense of loss and dread.

"If he is not in my hands within three days, I swear by almighty God, I will burn this forest to the ground until I find him. I will burn every farm, every hunting lodge, every village that calls itself Creek. I will kill your women and children and make you watch. Do you understand?"

Grimly, the four men nodded.

"Good." Jackson turned to Coffee. "Get them horses, or canoes if they prefer. Let's get this over with already."

As Coffee led away the prisoners, a soldier ran into the clearing, heading straight for Jackson. The general rubbed his eyes with his thumb and finger. He felt like trampled manure, and looked far worse. He needed food, drink, and, above all, a good night's sleep.

But a commander's work was never done.

"What is it, private?" he asked.

"The surgeon's tent, sir. Doctor Malloy said you'd want to see him."

"Of course he did."

Jackson took a deep breath, straightened his back, and headed for his next duty.

CHAPTER 34

An Honorable End

Red Eagle woke to darkness. Moonlit clouds crept across a star-scattered sky. The air was thick with the smell of smoke.

The world spun around him as he sat up. Clutching his head, he found a bandage swathing one side. Another was wrapped around his chest. He tried to stand, but his body forced him to move slowly. The blankets and furs piles around him fell to the ground, along with his dizziness.

Three score of Creek faces stared back at him in the darkness. Their lost, haunted expressions told him everything he needed to know.

"Jackson demands your surrender," Menawa sat in a fireside hunch. "He says without it he will burn us all, and all our lands, too." He looked up, firelight dancing across eyes framed by shadow. "We cannot give you up. You are all the hope we have left."

Looking around, Red Eagle knew one thing. Their hope was already lost. The only chance they had for life lay in his surrender.

"My bladder aches," he said.

No one was going to stop their war leader relieving himself. He walked away through the trees, safe in the knowledge that no one would think to stop him.

∽

The American camp was easy to find in the darkness. Its fires roared, illuminating the forest. A racket of voices sounded around the blaze, and the clink of bottles told Red Eagle celebration was at hand. This was no muted campfire hoping to conceal their location, this was a damned inferno. He wished they would respect the trees and conserve the wood, but he had lost the war. There would be no stopping these garish men. Jackson had threatened to burn it all to the ground, but at this rate, perhaps his men would do it for him.

The flicker of campfire made sneaking past the sentries more difficult, but Red Eagle hugged the shadows in the distance, surveying the weakest point. He knew full well that if any sentry spotted an Indian, he was as good as dead, even if he believed Jackson might let him live. Clad in nothing but bandages and buckskin trousers, his every hair standing on end, he crept through the forest beyond the edge of firelight until he spotted a shadowy opening between tents. Laughter and merriment from the fire was all the cover he needed, and he crawled closer. In an instant, he darted for the gap.

A mess of tents were arranged outward from the central fire. He inched, silently, carefully, around one, and rushed to the next before jumping across a gap to a wagon, finding cover of the shadow beneath it. He spied a large tent that stood above all the others. It had no stains, and guards were posted at both its front and back entrances.

Jackson's tent.

He lunged forward, one hand clutching his bandaged chest. One more tent to go. Drawing the knife from his belt, Red Eagle placed it between his teeth. He settled to the ground and slid on his belly through the dirt, low enough to avoid the attention of the guards. His wounds panged with sharp pains, but he knew it would all be over soon.

He arrived at the blind side of the tent, and rolled himself next to the canvas. He remembered the knife being sharper, but then again, he had killed a lot of Americans. He inhaled, and stuck it into the bottom of the tent, pausing to listen for alarm. The coast was clear. He quietly sawed through the fabric, and worked his way through a couple of ropes. The opening was big enough, and he slid under the edge of the tent. He was inside.

The last remains of a candle burned on a table in one corner. On the bed beside it, Andrew Jackson lay asleep. Clutching the knife in front of him, Red Eagle crept through the darkness until he crouched beside the sleeping general. He laid the blade against Jackson's throat.

"General Jackson," he whispered straight into the white man's ear.

Jackson's eyes shot open. He turned his head, then stopped as he felt the knife against his skin.

"Mister Weatherford," Jackson spoke as quietly as Red Eagle. "Make it quick. I detest long speeches."

In a blink, Red Eagle removed the knife from Jackson's throat and laid it beside the candle. Jackson's eyes widened with surprise.

"I'll give you your life," Red Eagle said, "if you grant me one condition. I'll surrender, and you let my people go. Grant them safe passage to join our sister tribes of the Seminole in Florida. All of them."

"You ask a great deal."

"A deal for your life." Red Eagle pointed at the knife. "Tell me, what does that cost?"

Something stirred at the far end of the tent. The canvas moved and a guard looked in.

"General Jackson, sir? Are you all right? We thought we heard—"

Red Eagle could tell the very moment the guard's eyes adjusted to the darkness. He stiffened, took a deep breath, and lunged forward.

"Indian!" he yelled. "There's an Indian in the general's tent!"

Other guards burst in, one of them carrying a lantern. They grabbed hold of Red Eagle and dragged him outside, trailing him through the mud to the center of the camp.

The place burst to life, men rushing out of their tents to see what the commotion was. A slender officer with floppy hair and arched eyebrows strode out to meet them.

"What is this?" the officer asked.

"An Indian, General Coffee, sir," one of the guards said. "Caught him with a knife in General Jackson's tent. Must be an assassin."

"I see," Coffee said. "Tie him to the flagpole, assemble the firing squad."

"Yes, sir."

The guards hauled Red Eagle, kicking and flailing, up against the flag post in the center of the camp. He did not protest as they tied his hands above his head, and wrapped ropes around his body. He couldn't escape from this.

Red Eagle looked up at the sky. A great star seemed to wink at him, and he saw Sapoth holding their son, smiling, walking straight for him. Death would soon take him, but at least they'd be together again. Peace, at last.

Soldiers stepped around Red Eagle, taunting him, spitting at him, licking their lips. How quickly they abandoned their celebration for the chance to see blood.

Coffee spotted General Jackson emerge from his tent. The commander was in his nightshirt with a coat draped over his shoulders. He was the only calm man there. The two men looked at Red Eagle and then back at each other.

Another figure appeared. A long skirt danced like river rapids as Mary Stiggins flew straight for Red Eagle, throwing her arms around his face. The soldiers stared in surprise as she gazed deep into his eyes. She nodded at him, and turned to shield him from the firing squad.

"General Jackson," she called out. "Please do not do this. Red Eagle is no monster. He's a good man."

"Quite right, Mrs. Stiggins," Jackson said. "I was just telling General Coffee the same thing."

The army parted to let the General through. Even in his nightshirt, with his hands thrust deep into the pockets of his coat, he was an impressive figure, his eyes bright and his gaze unwavering. No one laughed at the sight of his absurd outfit, which Jackson thought rather odd. Men saluted as he passed.

"Whatever else you might be, Mister Weatherford, you do not strike me as a murderer. Else I'd already be dead. A killer? Yes, so is every man here. That's the nature of our business. Dark is the mind who takes another's life. I admire your cunning. Even in the shadow of defeat, you're able to sneak past my army, into my tent, and bring a knife to my throat. You're a man of audacity, too, but that's not what I want to know."

Standing a foot away from Red Eagle, he looked him in the eye.

"Tell me, Mister Weatherford. Are you a man of your word?" Jackson asked, studying Red Eagle's expression.

"Yes," Red Eagle said.

Jackson's eyes scanned his face for any hint of untruth. The collective held its breath in silence. An owl hooted in the distance. Jackson removed Red Eagle's knife from his pocket, and examined the blade.

"I believe you," he returned the prisoner's gaze. "Free passage for your people in exchange for your word that you'll never make war again."

The end of war. Red Eagle had never wanted it in the first place. He had fought, and failed, for peace time and time again. Finally, the fever of violence had burned out. The prophets were gone and with them their temper.

"Yes," he said at last.

"Very well." Jackson labored to cut Red Eagle free from his bonds, and handed him his knife. "You should keep this sharper."

The ropes fell away and Red Eagle stood, face to face with his deadliest opponent.

"Your people have safe passage," Jackson said. "I have the power to pardon you. I'll give you your life, Red Eagle, since you gave me mine."

CHAPTER 35

To Live with Peace

The summer sun beat down on Red Eagle's shoulders. This was the first time he had been able to revisit the site where his trading post once stood. Where his family once lived. It took time to arrange for passage back here.

The Americans took half of the Creek lands in the treaty. Those who wished safe passage to Florida and their cousin tribe, the Seminoles, were allowed. Those who wished to return home were also allowed, and the lands Creek men had obtained by the white man's rules—which they called 'private property'—were honored, their ownership upheld. That included the lands belonging to Red Eagle.

Finally, he was home.

The last time he had been here, his entire life laid in blazing ruin. His life made whole by a woman's love only remained in charred scars across the landscape. They represented the only tie to the happiest moments in his life. And also, the empty sense of dread from his very worst. It was where he belonged.

Rounding the familiar bend in the Coosa river, the clearing opened up before him.

He stopped, mouth agape. Instead of ruins, there stood a house grander than the one he had lived in before. A barn stood on one side beside a stable for horses. The ground floor of the house had big shop windows. The signs of a trader.

A small crowd stood in front of the house. Tears of joy ran down Red Eagle's face as he approached. Men and women, natives and whites, Lower and Upper Creek. Friends he had thought forever torn apart.

At the front stood Mary Stiggins.

"Everyone here is someone you saved. From massacre or imprisonment or some other awful fate. You saved us all, so we built this for you. It's time to stop being a warrior and become a trader again."

"This is too much, I..." Red Eagle stood before the structure.

"And one more thing."

Linking her arm through his, Mary led him up the front steps of his new home. The front door swung open and McIntosh, his arm in a sling, gingerly stepped out into the light of day.

"Thought you'd seen the last of me, didn't you?" McIntosh said and Red Eagle leaped to wrap his arms around his friend, who winced in pain. "Easy, not fully healed yet."

"As long as you had no part in building the house, it must be well built."

The two laughed and took seats on the porch overlooking the river, ready to talk the afternoon away.

∽

The old gray mare stood in the stable's corner stall. She

earned the place of honor, saving Red Eagle's life in the leap at the Holy Ground. Now he visited her each day to reward her with oats and tenderness. They were both nearing retirement.

"It's been a good month, old girl," he brushed her mane. "Sold all our flour. Sent a boatload of pelts to the city and got a good sum back in return. I think—"

"Mind if I interrupt?" Mary asked from the door of the barn, holding the tiny hand of their daughter. A stone flew behind her as their son kicked it toward a bale of hay. "There's a man here to see you. Says it's important."

Setting aside the brush, Red Eagle gave Mary and the children a hug and a kiss each.

"You are never an interruption," he kissed her and beamed into her eyes with happiness. "Let's see what's so important."

He strolled through sunshine to the porch of his store. A fresh-faced man stood there, smiling thoughtfully as he looked out across the river. There was something familiar about him, though Red Eagle couldn't place it.

"William Weatherford," Red Eagle held out his right hand. "At your service."

The man held out his left hand.

"Sorry," he nodded to the empty sleeve where his right arm should have been. "I lost it in the war. Robert Harding, aide to Andrew Jackson."

"Captain Harding!" Red Eagle exclaimed. "Of course!"

"Not captain anymore," Harding gave a sad smile. "Not without my sword arm, but General Jackson was good enough to help me find another career."

"How is the general?" Red Eagle asked.

"He's running for political office," Harding laughed. "If you can believe it. Why I'm here, actually. He was hoping you might visit him as a guest of honor in Tennessee, remind people about his ability to forge peace in times of war.

"Might be just an excuse, though. This campaign has him reflecting over old times. Suspect he's yearning to talk with you again."

∽

Like commanding an army, running for office never seemed to stop. Jackson finished the speech some time ago, glad-handing and charming would-be voters as workers brought down the banners and rolled up the ribbons. Finally, Jackson was alone in the town square. What a relief, this solitude. But he had guests waiting. No time to waste, as he exited the town green toward the tavern on the corner. The sound of his boots marching along the dirt road filled the square, his pace subconsciously finding the rhythm of a military march.

Harding waited for him on the steps outside. With a nod, he ushered Jackson inside, settling him in a room in the back. Several familiar faces awaited.

Red Eagle and his former war compatriot Menawa sat on one side. On the other, McIntosh and his former ally Major Ridge of the Cherokee. Jackson pulled up a chair at the end of the booth.

"How long has it been," Jackson said. "Ten years?"

Jackson smiled, pulling cigars from his pocket to offer around the table. He found no takers. Pushing the rest into his pocket, he put one to his lips and lit it with a lantern. Dusk was falling across the large frontier town. Its well-to-do church, freshly built town square, and full stables had all the makings of a promising future. The saloon was full.

"Do you think you'll win?" McIntosh asked.

"Hope so. But who can say?"

"You would have great power," Red Eagle contemplated a nation run by Jackson.

"Perhaps." Jackson blew a long stream of smoke. "But will that feeling ever eclipse that of war? We didn't take the easy way to get there, but like it or not, you all helped stop a bad situation from getting much worse. Found peace against an impossible tide.

"This nation isn't about settlers and natives. It's about what happens when they come together. When we started that war, I hated you sons of bitches. Thought your kind was no better than dogs. We tore each other apart, but I learned then and there, these lands weren't worth having unless we brought us all back together."

"We are not all back together." Menawa stared stone-faced at Jackson. "The terms remain unequal. I have no reason to believe it will ever be fair."

"The terms are unequal, you're right," Jackson said. "That brings me to why I invited you here. I want to forge a new treaty, and I ask you to help me as my partners. Let's make one to stand the test of time."

The four men in the booth traded uneasy glances and shifted in their seats.

"What did you have in mind?" Ridge asked.

"Let me win this thing and then we'll talk details. For now, I just want you to know that I trust you. Respect you. My most precious contacts among the Five Civilized Tribes. I hope you trust me, too."

There was light nodding and a hint of agreement among the men and they stood to remove themselves from the booth. As the other men sauntered toward the exit, Jackson held Red Eagle back. "The world we've made. Is it so bad?"

"When a Creek man is president, perhaps ask me then." Red Eagle's taut face was not unkind.

"You should run," Jackson grinned. "But not for 8 years. I'd hate to lose."

Red Eagle shook his head. "One campaign was enough for me. Don't have the stomach for it."

"Fair," Jackson said. "And I dare say it makes my life easier."

"Why?"

"What you stand for. The bridge between two worlds," Jackson paused while he took a long, thoughtful drag on his cigar. "Your people must learn to reconcile the changing tides in this great land. Not just the Creeks. All the tribes. The United States will continue to expand, and I'd like to do so in peace. Hope those tribes feel the same."

"You're going to take more lands?" Red Eagle's face fell. "Push more out of their homes?"

"I can't stop the march of progress," Jackson said. "Neither can you. There will be farms and towns all across this continent. Whole place will be happier, more prosperous. We call that America. My hope is that this new treaty will provide growth and safety for all. Hope no traditionalists stand in the way."

Red Eagle stared sadly out the window of the tavern, thinking of all those people Jackson had labeled as traditionalists. Men and women, old and young, a peaceful life that would be ripped and torn and cut in the name of what Jackson calls America. Through the window, the late afternoon sun glared bright red, as if there was fire on the horizon.

"And if the tribes don't share your idea of progress?"

"We will remove them," Jackson said. "Humanely, of course. Find them another place to live. Somewhere out West where no one will bother them."

As much as he respected Jackson as a battle commander, the man was blind to the darkness of his schemes. No white man would remove a native peacefully. There was too much hatred, and he could feel it staring at him around the saloon. There would be pain ahead, of that Red Eagle was sure.

"If I can't count on you to talk some sense into your people," Jackson said, "then I hope McIntosh and Ridge will. I'm afraid, after our little war, not everyone in your neck of the woods respects them."

Red Eagle was silent.

"Let me buy you a drink. Talk it over." Jackson moved to the bar and gestured for Red Eagle to follow. Ordering two glasses of whiskey, Jackson slid one over to Red Eagle and offered a toast. "To progress." Jackson raised his glass.

Red Eagle did not smile. He feared Jackson now more than ever. The statesman's uniform was more dangerous than the general's. Red Eagle was an old man now. His fighting days were done. This was not the life he had hoped for before the war. It wasn't the peace his people spilled blood for, either. But it was the life he had been given. It would not be his fight to challenge Jackson, yet again. That was a battle with even less hope for victory.

Red Eagle tipped the glass back. Jackson smiled, his eyes never leaving Red Eagle's, and did the same.

Red Eagle stepped back from the bar, with Jackson's eyes still fixed on him, and spouted the whiskey out onto the floor of the tavern in a long thin stream. He closed his eyes and imagined he was hundreds of miles away, a lifetime ago, feeling the burn of the whiskey in his mouth like the warmth of the Puskita's fire, and the gaze from Sapoth from the bench of the square ground. He tilted his head back and imagined the last White Drink, so long ago, pouring out onto the Square Ground floor.

The memory was intensely personal, yet felt bigger than him at the same time. The kind of memory that transcends a man, and lives in dreams or on the winds of the Breathmaker.

Red Eagle opened his eyes, gazing straight past Andrew Jackson, wiped his mouth, and dropped the whiskey glass on the ground. It shattered on the hardwood floor, sending sparkling shards dancing in the red sunlight like the embers of a sacred fire.

Jackson was frozen. He didn't know how to interpret the gesture, but before he could compose himself, Red Eagle had swung out the tavern door.

This would be the last time they saw one another in this life.

∼

EPILOGUE

In 1824, Red Eagle, or William Weatherford, died in his home in Monroe County, Alabama.

In 1825, William McIntosh signed the Treaty of Indian Springs with the United States government, ceding most of the remaining Creek ancestral lands in exchange for cash and territory in present-day Oklahoma and Arkansas. This treaty was immediately declared fraudulent by the Creek National Council, who ruled that ceding communal lands without authority was a capital crime. Under orders from the council, Menawa led a group of warriors to McIntosh's land, where they burned his home, then shot and stabbed him to death.

In 1829, Andrew Jackson was elected President of the United States, popularized largely by his military exploits against the Native Americans and British in the Southeastern U.S. The founder of the Democratic Party, Jackson sought to advance the rights of the "common man".

In 1835, under strong pressure from President Jackson, Major Ridge signed the Treaty of New Echota, ceding the remainder of Cherokee ancestral lands to the U.S. for cash and western territory. Terms called for the Cherokee to vacate their lands by the end of 1837.

In 1837, Menawa died while being removed from the ancient Creek lands to Oklahoma.

In 1838, the U.S. forcibly rounded up the remaining Cherokee living on tribal lands in the Southeast and led them on a march toward Oklahoma. This journey, which caused the death of over 4,000 Cherokee, became known as "The Trail of Tears."

In 1839, the Cherokee National Council found Ridge personally responsible for the deaths along "The Trail of Tears" and he was executed in accordance with the Cherokee Blood Law, within the borders of the new tribal lands of Oklahoma.

In 1858, the last descendants of the Creek lineage concluded the final Seminole War and agreed to relocate from Florida to the Indian Territory in return for cash and safe passage. Several hundred Seminole refused and retreated deep into the Everglades, never to surrender to the U.S. government.

Printed in Great Britain
by Amazon